THE STORY OF CREATION:
A COMPILATION

THE STORY OF CREATION: A COMPILATION

Dr. Joshua David Stone

Writers Club Press
San Jose   New York   Lincoln   Shanghai

The Story of Creation: A Compilation

Writers Club Press
an imprint of iUniverse, Inc.

For information address:
iUniverse, Inc.
5220 S. 16th St., Suite 200
Lincoln, NE 68512
www.iuniverse.com

ISBN: 0-595-20941-6

Printed in the United States of America

Contents

1

The Story of Creation

I have written extensively in my book *The Complete Ascension Manual* on how everyone has an Oversoul or Higher Self that is in charge of 12 Souls that incarnate in different worlds to gain Love, Wisdom, Power and Virtue for the development of the Oversoul. Each person also has 12 Oversouls that make up the Monad, or Mighty I Am Presence. This means that each person is made up of 144 Souls in the Monadic, or Mighty I Am Presence, family soul, so to speak.

I have also written extensively in my book *Cosmic Ascension* about the importance of integrating and cleansing Soul Extensions or Souls, not only from one's Oversoul and Monad, but also from one's Monadic Group connections. In other words, as one evolves beyond the Monad, one forms group consciousness networks or modules. It is also possible to integrate and cleanse Soul Extensions from these Monadic Modules, hypothetically, all the way back to Source! This is one of the many keys to accelerating evolution!

It must be understood that the nature of God is consciousness. God is, in a sense, the Omniversal Soul! If you think about what Creation is, it is God just splitting His omniversal consciousness into forms. God breathes them out, or Big Bangs them out, in one mighty conscious breath and a

Day, or hundred million-year cycle, of Brahma, and then breathes them back in. A Cosmic Day and a Cosmic Night. God takes smaller breaths for each universe and one bigger breath for all universes. God creates the Cosmic Monads, which might also be called "God Cells"! Each of these 12 God Cells, or Cosmic Monads, contain infinite numbers of Monads, or Mighty I Am Presences. Then these Monads, and/or Mighty I Am Presences, go out into Creation and each creates 12 Oversouls or Higher Selves. Each of these Oversouls and/or Higher Selves then goes out and creates 12 Souls, which is what we are. We are each one soul who has incarnated from our Oversoul. So, you see, my friends, God splits His consciousness to create the God Cell, or Cosmic Monad, which splits its consciousness to create the infinite numbers of individualized Monads, which splits its consciousness to each create 12 Oversouls, which splits its consciousness to create 12 Souls that incarnate on different planets and different dimensions to evolve the Oversoul, which is evolving the Monad, or Mighty I Am Presence, which is evolving the Group Modules of Monads, which is evolving the Cosmic Monad, or God Cells, which are evolving to Ascend God!

Now everyone is focusing on their individual Ascension, which is fine and appropriate, however, from a group consciousness lens, which can also be looked at simultaneously, there is only one Ascension and that is God Ascension! We are all the Eternal Self, or incarnations of God, or Aspects of God's Consciousness, being breathed back to God. It is all God's play. There are no separate individuals. We are all just "different kinds of flowers" in the Garden of God. There are three lineages of "flowers," however, these are: Ascended Master, Angelic, and Elohim; however, at the end, even they all become one! There are different races of Extraterrestrial beings, like the Adam Kadmon form, the Grays, the insect-looking ones, the lizard races, the cat race, the list is infinite, but these are all just different incarnations of God and/or different flowers of God in the Garden of God! Do you see, my beloved readers, it is just God splitting His consciousness into infinite forms? We are all Gods, serving other Gods, returning back to GOD the Creator! Do you see how silly war is, or competition, jealousy, or selfishness? For there are no beings but God. People get caught up in the form of things and do not see the essence behind all forms. Flowers do not compete. Daisies do not fight with roses or lilies! It is all just God's Play and Drama. The Divine Plan and unique thing about our return home is that GOD wants his incarnations of Self to return home "Conscious"! In other words, to return home to our true identity in GOD, out of our free choice, not because He forces us to! So, do you see, my friends, that all Creation is just the splitting of God's Consciousness down the evolutionary ladder! This is just the hierarchical structure of things, which is done so each level, in a sense, has a personal teacher to help them back up through the 352 levels back to GOD!

This is why Unconditional Love is so important, for it is all GOD! This is why sharing is so important, for it is all GOD! This is why seeing beyond appearances and form is so important while still being able to live in form and master form! This is why integration and balance is so important to learn at each level as we move up the evolutionary dimensional ladder of consciousness. My Beloved Readers, you have been given a Spiritual Vision here of Creation from the Full Spectrum Prism Lens of God! Where we focus on evolving our selves, God is focusing on evolving universes, Where we are working with ourselves, our students and our planet to become Integrated Spiritual Masters, GOD is the Supreme Integrated Spiritual Master in charge of bringing all Creation into balance and integration within his Supreme Cosmic Body! The Elohim, the Cosmic and Planetary Ascended Masters, the Archangels and Angels, and the Christed Extraterrestrials are his agents throughout His Omniverse to help create this change. We are his agents on Earth at this time to create this change.

Once we achieve Christ Realization on a Planetary Level, we work on achieving being Solar Christs. Then Galactic Christs. Then Universal Christs! Then Multiuniversal Christs! Then Cosmic Christs! There is no skipping levels. One must serve at each level and master and integrate that level before being allowed to move back up to the next! There are 352 levels of Initiation, and, hence, 352 levels of Light Body to anchor and integrate! There are 352 levels of consciousness to master! Each of these 352 levels is also connected to a chakra system that must be anchored, activated, and actualized! GOD's Personality is made up of the 12 Great Cosmic Rays. Hence, we on Earth must learn to balance our Seven Rays on Earth and ultimately our Cosmic Rays, as well as everything else! Oneness and integration cannot be separated, for ultimately they are one in the same thing! Mastery, integration, and balance must be achieved at each level before one is allowed by the Grace of God and the Masters to move to the next! One must fully embody each level, demonstrate each level, and serve at each level before being allowed to move to the next! Each level one achieves is an initiation or ascension of sorts to the next level. The key is that it must not only be done in your Spiritual body, it must also be "integrated" into your mental, emotional, etheric, physical and Earthly self and vehicle as well, as long as one has a physical/Earthly aspect to work with and through!

The Story of Creation on Earth and the Garden of Eden

There was a time on Earth during the time of the ancient civilization of Lemuria (which predated Atlantis) when the God/Goddess energies were in perfect balance! In the Bible, this could be referred to as the time of the Garden of Eden, or first Golden Age on this planet! However, when there was the first eating of the fruit from the "Tree of Good and Evil," this Biblical story speaks to that time when man, for the first time on Earth, misused his free choice and thought out of harmony with GOD! This, of course, was the beginning of negative ego/fear-based/separative thinking and feeling! This was the first time mankind thought out of harmony with GOD and out of harmony with the Spiritual/Christ/Buddha consciousness!

It was this choice of fear, separation, selfishness, lower-self desire, conditional love, judgment, anger, grudges, guilt, hurt, depression, and sadness that also began the process of rejection and abuse of the Divine Mother and Goddess energies on Earth!

This misuse of free choice also began a process of mass consciousness on the Earth to identify with masculine energies over feminine energies! The mind over the heart! Thinking over intuition! Thinking over feeling! Thinking over psychic perceptions! Thinking and science over Spirituality! Thinking, selfishness and technology over anything in regard to Mother Earth and Nature!

My Beloved Readers, this caused an over-identification with the Patriarchy over the Matriarchy! Left brain became more important than right brain! Men began to control society and women were not seen as equals! This over-identification with masculine energy caused there to be too much aggressiveness, willfulness, loss of sensitivity, psychological and physical violence, inability to nurture, pridefulness, loss of compassion, jealousy, competition, loss of unconditional love, and a focus on war as a means to get what one wanted!

There became a focus on science and technology over Spirituality and Mother Earth. Nothing was considered real unless you could experience it with your five physical senses! Logic was favored over intuition, channeling, or psychic perception! There was the rejection and disowning of the 22 Supersenses of GOD that go beyond the five physical senses!

The following story of Creation is quite an amazing and often unbelievable story. I just want to qualify this by saying that I didn't make any of this up myself. All of this information comes directly out of the Universal Mind channelings of myself, Edgar Cayce, and other sources such as Djwhal Khul, Ruth Montgomery, The Tibetan Foundation, and other similar types of channelings. The amazing thing is that all these different sources tell a similar story, so I know that I am very much on the mark, although some of it may be quite surprising to some readers.

*   *   *

In the beginning was one source of Light, the one presence called God. God, in His great joy and love, had a desire to create, to express Himself. From this undifferentiated state, God created suns, moons, galaxies, and universes. He liked what He had created. Something, however, was missing—companionship. God wanted to create self-conscious beings that could share His joy of creation. Out of the infinity of God came trillions of sparks of Light made in His image.

Out of this expression also came Amilius, the Light, the first expression of the Divine mind, the first manifestation of Spirit. All souls were created in the beginning and all souls were androgynous. The unique thing about our creation was the aspect of free choice.

In our creation, we went jetting out into the universe, creating as God creates, with our minds, and extending God's kingdom. We were perfect, and this was the Edenic state. In our travels through the infinity of God, we discovered the physical, or material, universe and we were intrigued, for in the beginning we didn't have physical bodies, just spiritual bodies.

Then we began projecting a part of ourselves into, let's say, the Earth, to explore the beauty of matter. There was, in actuality, nothing wrong with this, for the entire infinite universe was a playground of sorts. We began projecting a part of ourselves into a tree to see what a tree was like. Then we would project ourselves into a rock to see what that was like, then into an animal to experience what it was like to eat grass and interrelate with other animals.

In each case, we would do this and then we would leave and project ourselves back into the spiritual planes. We would also, then, with the incredible power of our minds, create thoughtforms of animals through the power of our imaginations. These thoughtforms would begin to densify and we would inhabit these thoughtform creatures just as we would an animal that had already been created.

This was all fine until that moment in Creation that the Bible refers to as "the fall of man." It was in this moment that we forgot who we were because of our over-identification with the material universe. We got caught in the density of matter, and thought we were the animals or thoughtform animal creatures we had created.

Falling under the illusion that we were material instead of spiritual in identity began the downward spiral of Creation. In this moment, "ego" began, ego being a thought system and philosophy based on the illusion-ary belief in separation, fear, selfishness, and death.

This phenomenon of souls getting more and more deeply caught up in the illusion of matter continued at an alarming rate. Amilius (an incarna-tion of Jesus) and other higher beings who had not fallen, knew that something had to be done to help their fellow brothers and sisters, for man was continuing to create a conglomeration of monstrosities to satisfy his out of control desire.

He created cyclopes, satyrs, centaurs, unicorns, animal bodies with human heads, beings with hooves, claws, feathers, wings, and tails. Man had become trapped in the grotesque bodies that were not suitable for sons and daughters of God. Man even created the first female, whose name was Lilith, and who was the forerunner of Eve. This projection was created to satisfy his selfish carnal desires.

The plan that God and the Godforce created to rectify this situation was the creation of five physical races on the five continents of the planet. Each race had a different skin color. No skin color was better than another was, but each was for a different climate condition. Certain skin colors were better suited for certain climates.

The plan was that all those souls who were caught up in matter would use these more perfectly fitted human bodies to incarnate into, bodies that were more fitting for sons and daughters of God.

After the creation of the five races, there were one hundred thirty-three million souls on the Earth. The red race lived in Atlantis and America, the brown race in the Andes and Lemuria, the yellow race in the Gobi Desert of East Asia, the black race in the Sudan and upper West Africa, and the white race in Iran along the Black Sea and in the Carpathian Mountains of central Europe.

The basic plan that God created was reincarnation: souls would incarnate into these human bodies rather than into animal bodies to reawaken to their true identity as God-beings and learn to demonstrate this on Earth, hence beginning their ascent back to the Creator.

This act of creation occurred ten and a half million years ago. The animal influences created by the fall and the initial thoughtform projections of animals didn't completely disappear from the Earth until around 9,000 B.C. Remnants of these pathetic creatures were later depicted in our mythology and in Assyrian and Egyptian art.

Another factor that involved the grotesque animal creations was that in the earliest of times, human beings were able to procreate with the animal species and with the grotesque beings. After human souls were separated into male and female, God imposed Divine laws making it impossible for human beings to produce offspring with another species.

Man was able to live up to one thousand years in the same body until another Divine law was implemented to change this because of the need for souls to be able to reflect more on the inner plane about the purpose and reason for incarnation.

Amilius himself descended into matter and became the first Adam at the time of the creation of the first five root races. Adam was the first of the perfected race, the first of the sons of God, as opposed to what the Bible refers to as the daughters of men. Adam was an individual but also a symbol of all five races, as was Eve.

The Seven Root Races

The following chart shows the seven root races that make up what is esoterically termed the "manvantara," or world cycle. These root races, seen in column one of the graph, make up a period of time of from eighteen and a half million years ago to our present day.

We are currently living in the Aryan root race. This term was completely distorted by Hitler and Nazi Germany, so please don't think of it in those terms. The Aryan race has been in existence for over a million years and will continue for some time more.

The Meruvian root race is just beginning to come into play, so there is kind of an overlapping of root races going on. The name of the seventh root race is the Paradisian.

I would also like to add that Djwhal Khul has told me that the first two root races, the Polarian and Hyperborean, are often referred to as the Pre-Lemurian root races, which is also how The Tibetan Foundation has referenced them. This is because the first two races were not completely physical as we understand physicality.

The continents on which these root races began and thrived on are listed in the second column. The third column lists the specific type of psychospiritual attunement each root race had. The fourth column lists the chakra each root race was working on developing. The fifth column lists the type of yoga each root race was practicing.

Tara, the continent for the final root race, is a continent that will emerge from the ocean floor in the distant future.

The members of the Polarian, or first, root race had huge filamentous bodies and were more etheric than physical. They were also totally sexless. They multiplied by a process of what scientists refer to as fission, or budding. For this reason, they were basically immortal. They have been called the "archetypal race." Their bodies were basically gaseous in nature.

The members of the Hyperborean, or second, root race were similar to the first, however, they slowly but surely began the process of materializing more. Djwhal Khul and The Tibetan Foundation have often just called these two root races "Pre-Lemurian," because they weren't totally physicalized as the members of the Lemurian, or third, root race were. Human beings as we know them, began with this third root race.

When human life first manifested on Earth in these first two root races, the only dry land was at the North Pole. The rest of the Earth was covered with water. This polar continent looked like a skullcap on the head of the Earth. This is the only continent that will never submerge under water in the entire manvantara, or world cycle, of all seven root races. One other interesting point is that Lemuria was called the "Land of Shalmali" at the time it existed.

It is also important to understand that the seven root races all have seven sub-races. This makes a total of forty-nine sub-races in a manvantara. An example of this can be shown by our present Aryan root race: the Hindu began sixty-two thousand years ago, the Arabian forty-two thousand years ago, the Iranian thirty-two thousand years ago, the Celtic twenty-two thousand years ago, the Teutonic twenty-two thousand years ago; the sixth and seventh sub-races of the Aryan root race are evolving in America and on a continent that will be arising in the Pacific Ocean. To make God's plan even more intricate, every sub-race race has seven family races, which I am not going to get into.

The Seven Root Races

Root Races	Continent	Attunement	Chakra	Yoga
1 Polarian	The Imperishable	Physical Attunement	1st Chakra	Hatha
2 Hyperborean	Continent of Hyperborea Sacred Land	Physical Attunement	1st Chakra	Hatha
3 Lemurian	Continent of Lemuria	Physical Attunement	2nd Chakra	Hatha
4 Atlantean	Continent of Atlantis	Emotional Attunement	3rd Chakra	Bhakti
5 Aryan	Europe, Asia Minor, America	Mental Attunement	4th Chakra	Raja
6 Meruvian	North America	Personality Integration	5th Chakra	Agni
7 Paradisian	Tara	Soul Attunement	6th Chakra	Unknown

Pre-Lemurian History

There were two great Avatars who came to Earth in the early Pre-Lemurian times. The first Avatar focused an energy of spiritual attunement on the Earth. He came forth as a scientist, through a highly developed civilization. His message was to blend the scientific and the spiritual understandings. Humanity didn't accept his message at the time. They weren't ready for it. So, this great teacher left. He has since returned into that full-fledged co-creator state.

Another great Avatar was sent to Earth at a later Pre-Lemurian time. He was a very tall man and he was fond of wearing a silver robe. He was the first great teacher who really made an impact on the Earth. His name was Lo Chi. Lo Chi anchored courage, wisdom, and love in their beginning stages. He took a war-torn civilization and began to build a spiritual community with temples all over the land. At the end of his reign, a mass ascension took place.

The next great teacher who came changed his approach and stressed the emotional qualities and occupations rather than the scientific, as the first Avatar had. Some of the greatest art was produced; however, the scientific side of society began to shut down. In a sense, a pendulum-swing took place, from a more masculine to a more feminine society. Great strides were made in art, music, and dance, but the mental creativity and potency were not there because of this pendulum-swing. This began to change over a long period of time and society became more balanced. Then another mass ascension took place.

Vywamus has called these two previous mass ascensions periods of spiritual harvesting. He says that we are again approaching a harvesting time in this century. This has to do with Sanat Kumara, who has reached another plateau in his cosmic evolution. Each time he reaches one of these plateaus it is time for the harvesting of souls, or mass ascension.

We are currently completing a six thousand-year, a twelve thousand-year, and a thirty-six thousand-year cycle. Each time two or more cycles come together, that period is extremely important. We are in that period now. This harvesting window is approximately one hundred years long. The end of this hundred-year cycle is from 1995 to the year 2012. The closer to the end of this hundred year cycle, the greater the harvesting. To be incarnated at this time in history is a very great opportunity!

The Electrical Wars

It was also in this Pre-Lemurian period that planet Earth was attacked by the "Electrical Ones," a group of beings from another planet who wanted to take it over. Humanity began to defend itself, and this war lasted for five hundred years. Earthlings eventually won this battle. The Electrical Ones were not really evil, but simply scientists looking for a new place to live. They came from a very great distance. This war is part of the fear of spaceships that still exists to this day in the race consciousness, for these Electrical Ones took people and animals aboard spaceships and did painful experiments on them. A lot of our present-day fixations and patterns of attack/defense programming stem from this period in the Earth's history.

The Electrical Ones were actually seeking to bring their technology of Light to the planet to aid in the trip back to the Source. Humanity and the Earth, however, were moving toward greater material density. This was not a negative thing on the part of the Earth. The Earth and humanity were saying that they wanted to learn everything they could within the densest part of physicality.

A truce was finally declared after five hundred years of war and many of the Electrical Ones left, promising to return when the Earth was ready. Some stayed in specific areas given to them. The Electrical Ones stimulated an impatience for this downward materialistic cycle.

Lemuria

Lemuria, or Mu, was a landmass lying in the Pacific Ocean and extending from the United States all the way to South America. The Lemurian stage of existence had to do with the race consciousness learning the lesson of physical attunement. Humanity, as a whole, progresses in stages, and physical attunement was the key lesson during this period of history.

The Lemurians were very philosophical and spiritual people, much more so than the Atlanteans, who were much more technologically advanced and focused.

At this period of history, great dinosaurs roamed the Earth and because of this, the Lemurians, to a great extent, had to live underground. They lived in caves, hiding from the dinosaurs except to hunt for food. They would beautifully and artistically decorate their caves. The Lemurians were rather small, physically: men were five feet tall and women a few inches shorter. The survival rate of children was not very high. They lived on grain, berries, and fruit.

Atlantis

Atlantis was in the north Atlantic Ocean. It compared in size to Europe and Russia combined. The eastern seaboard of the United States, then mostly under water, comprised the coastal lowlands of Atlantis, which extended from Mexico as far as the Mediterranean Sea.

As mentioned earlier, dinosaurs roamed the Earth during this time, and many of them were carnivorous. Many of the Atlanteans lived in great walled cities to protect themselves from these beasts.

Also still existing in Atlantis were the grotesque animal-like humans that I spoke of earlier in this chapter. By certain segments of the society they were called "things" and treated as slaves and beasts of burden. There were two groups of people in Atlantis: those who served the Law of One and those called the Sons of Belial.

The Sons of Belial were the followers of Beelzebub. They were the lords of materialism—the selfish, materialistic, and egotistical group. These people enslaved the "things," or animal-humans, that had hooves, claws, feathers, wings, or tails on human bodies.

Those people who served the Law of One tried to help the "things," both spiritually and physically, by taking them to the great temples of healing in Atlantis. Using advanced technologies of crystals, Light, and sound, they were often able to do surgery to remove the un-god-like appendages that no longer manifested the Adam Kadmon perfect design that God had created for the perfected human body.

In 52,000 B.C., a council of wisemen of the five races was convened to discuss ways to get rid of the dinosaurs. A plan to use super-potent chemical forces to poison the dinosaurs in their lairs was discussed. This plan was implemented and began to work.

The first of a series of three continental Earth-change catastrophes occurred about 50,700 B.C. This first catastrophe occurred as a result of the use of chemicals and explosives to annihilate the dinosaurs. Huge and numerous gas pockets were blown open in the lairs of the animals, which precipitated volcanic eruptions and earthquakes. The magnitude of the disturbances was so great that it caused the axis of the Earth to shift, bringing the poles to their present positions and causing the last great ice age.

The continent of Lemuria was destroyed, but strangely enough, Atlantis was not affected that much in terms of its landmass. Lemuria's entire continent sank to the bottom of the ocean because of the pole shift. Atlantis then became the premiere civilization on the planet. As mentioned earlier, Atlantis was very technologically advanced but much less spiritually advanced, much like the United States is today. In fact, many of the same souls who lived in Atlantis are reincarnated and living in the United States today.

The great cataclysm destroyed most of the dinosaurs because of the landmass transformation and the change in climate conditions. Atlantis now being the premiere civilization on the planet, began to thrive. It was during this period that Extraterrestrials visited Atlantis and introduced them to advanced crystal technology.

The Atlanteans used crystal energy to run almost every aspect of society. They had one great crystal that was the major energy source for the entire continent. It ran cars, ships, submarines, and airplanes, providing all the energy needs of the society. Science was more and more becoming the new god, and people became less and less interested in the presence of God.

The Sons of Belial and negative Extraterrestrial influences began to take more and more control over Atlantean civilization. The crystal energy began to be used for warfare and to control the people. One fateful day, Atlantean scientists tried to use the great crystal to send some kind of energy beam through the Earth's crust for some evil purpose. This precipitated a massive explosion, the likes of which had never before been seen on this planet. This occurred in approximately 28,000 B.C. and resulted in the submergence of Atlantis into three islands. This account was alluded to in the Bible story of Noah's Ark and the great flood.

A period of building began in Atlantis after this great catastrophe, but Atlantis never returned to its original glory. Atlantis became more and more decadent as time went on. There were great advancements in electricity, atomic power, and the harnessing of the sun's energy; however, the country reached its depths of moral and spiritual decline. Human sacrifice and sun-worshiping were prevalent, as were adultery and corruption.

The sun crystals were crudely adapted as a means of coercion, torture, and punishment. The common people called the many sun crystals the "44 terrible crystals." Gigantic Earth changes rocked Atlantis around 9,500 B.C. and Atlantis vanished from the face of the Earth. The explosion was one million times greater than that at Hiroshima.

Those Atlanteans serving the Law of One listened to God and the prophets and fled before this catastrophe occurred. They went to Egypt, and they later became known as the Mayans in the Yucatan and as the Iroquois Indians in America. In all these civilizations, the influence of Atlantis was felt in the building of pyramids.

All of the secrets of Atlantis are stored in the Hall of Records in the Great Pyramid. These records are mystically protected. Paul Solomon and Edgar Cayce, in their source channelings, have said that a great initiate who is now living on the planet, by the name of John of Penial (who is the reincarnation of John the Beloved, the disciple of Christ), will be the great one who will travel to Egypt and release all these records.

In the exodus from Atlantis to Egypt they took with them a great spiritual teacher whose name was Thoth. For several thousand years Thoth was incarnated in Egypt, which was a civilization of great spirituality. The pyramids were actually temples of initiation.

Vywamus has said that Egyptian history lasted as long as one hundred thousand years, not just the four thousand or five thousand years that modern historians speak of. Egypt had a great deal of Extraterrestrial involvement. The concept of the pyramid came from other planets. The Egyptian civilization was the blending of consciousness from several other planets.

Plato has referred to the sinking of Atlantis in his writings. It is quite amazing to me that our modern history books are so limited in their scope. Edgar Cayce predicted that Atlantis would rise again and emerge off the eastern coast of the United States around 1968 or 1969. The Bahaman Islands are remnants of the peaks of Poseidia, one of the islands that was left after the second Atlantean earthquake. Divers found underwater temples and ruins sixty feet below the water in 1968, just as Cayce predicted.

The Bermuda Triangle, according to three different sources of information I have found in my research, is actually the great crystal that I spoke of earlier, which has sunk to the bottom of the ocean. At certain times when the sun shines upon the ocean floor at a certain angle in relationship to the moon, this great crystal is activated. Anything that passes through its energy vortex during this activation is turned into antimatter and is disintegrated. This is why the Bermuda Triangle effects occur only on specialized occasions and not all the time.

The United States is now going through a testing period very similar to that of Atlantis fifty thousand years ago. The question is whether our development of science and technology is going to cause us to lose sight of our true reason for being here, which is a more spiritual one.

The Cosmic Day and the Creation of the Planet Earth

In this chapter about the story of creation, I have been focusing on the creation of human life on this planet. The chapter, however, would not be complete if I did not speak of the creation of Planet Earth herself. This gets into the understanding of the meaning of the Cosmic Day or a day in the life of Brahma (God).

One day in the life of Brahma equals four billion three hundred twenty million years. One night in the life of Brahma equals four billion three hundred twenty million years.

One twenty-four hour day in the life of Brahma equals eight billion six hundred forty million years. Three hundred sixty full days make up one year of Brahma, which equals three trillion one hundred ten billion four hundred million years.

One hundred years constitute the whole period of Brahma's age (Maha Kalpa), three hundred eleven trillion forty billion years.

Monads

According to Djwhal Khul, God created sixty thousand million monads in our planetary system. Each monad creates twelve souls, and each soul creates twelve soul extensions or incarnated personalities. Multiply sixty thousand million times one hundred forty-four and you have the number of people working through this school. Djwhal has also stated that of these sixty thousand million monads, thirty-five thousand million monads are of the second ray of love, twenty thousand million monads are of activity, or the third ray, and five thousand million monads are of power, or the first ray.

More on the Life of Brahma

At the end of one Cosmic Day, all of creation for that particular source is consumed and called back into Source. Then there is a cosmic night before the impetus of the creation of another Cosmic Day.

You will be interested to know that in the Cosmic Day of which Earth is a part, 3.1 billion years have already gone by. We need not worry. We still have 1.2 billion years left in our present Cosmic Day. Human life as we know it has existed on Planet Earth in its present physical form for only 10.5 million years. We still have 1.2 billion years left.

This whole process, on a cosmic scale, is known as the in-breath and out-breath of Brahma (later in this book, I have written a chapter by this title); it signifies a smaller cycle that the Earth is experiencing within the larger cosmic understanding of these cycles of the in-breaths and out-breaths of God.

2

The Great Secret of the Seven Golden Ages on Earth

My Beloved Readers, when one of the great secrets of the ages has to do with the understanding that we are now moving into the Seventh Golden Age, the great unknown secret is, "What were the previous six Golden Ages?" For your enjoyment and edification, I asked Spirit and the inner plane Ascended Masters this question and this is what I was told!

First Golden Age: Paradise (Early Etheric Lemuria)
Second Golden Age: Lemuria
Third Golden Age: Atlantis
Fourth Golden Age: Ancient Egypt and the Pyramids
Fifth Golden Age: Mayan Civilization
Sixth Golden Age: Ancient Greece
Seventh Golden Age: Present Aquarian Age we are now moving into

First Golden Age: Paradise (Early Etheric Lemuria)

This First Golden Age was in earlier Lemuria, or Mu, which was a major continent in the Pacific Ocean region. In this earliest period of

Earth's history, the Earth was etheric in nature and not physical in a third-dimensional sense as it is now. This is what the Bible referred to as the "Garden of Eden," prior to the eating of the apple from the Tree of Knowledge. This was the First Golden Age and a time when all was in Spiritual/Christ/Buddha perfection and which predated the movement into separation on this planet. This is the state of consciousness we are now in the movement back towards!

Second Golden Age: Lemuria

This Second Golden Age was in later Lemuria after the eating of the apple from the Tree of Knowledge. The eating of this apple set in motion the movement into separation that led eventually to the etheric nature of this planet moving into a more third-dimensional dense state! Interestingly enough, this was not part of the original Divine Plan! The Earth was not supposed to become as dense as it has. This was the reason for the plan of reincarnation, which was instituted to rectify this problem. So, third-dimensionally-physicalized Lemuria was the Second Golden Age!

Third Golden Age: Atlantis

The Third Golden Age was Atlantis. This was a continent in the Atlantic Ocean off Bermuda that was much more technologically advanced than Lemuria, which was a little more agricultural in nature. Atlantis was an extremely advanced civilization that was much more technologically advanced than our present civilization. The entire energy supply was run by Crystal energy. They had flying cars and flying ships. Unfortunately, however, they were unable to control the emotional body and negative ego, which eventually caused them to misuse their technology and destroy themselves in a series of three major cataclysmic events that sank Atlantis to the bottom of the ocean!

Fourth Golden Age: Ancient Egypt and the Pyramids

The Fourth Golden Age was ancient Egypt and the Pyramids. Thoth/Hermes was the great leader of Atlantis. The seers and prophets prophetically saw the destruction of Atlantis coming and the Spiritual Masters and high level initiates left and went to Egypt and the Mayan civilizations. This led to the Fourth Golden Age in Egypt. Here, Extraterrestrials from Sirius and Mars, among others, came and helped these Atlantean Masters build the Great House of Light known as the Great Pyramid of Giza, and the Sphinx. In the Sphinx in the Hall of Records are stored all the Atlantean information and mysteries that are being kept and protected mystically until mankind reaches a level of consciousness to have all this information unveiled again. The Great Pyramid was, of course, a place of Initiation in the highest sense of the term. This continued for a time until this civilization fell as well, in a Spiritual sense!

Fifth Golden Age: Mayan Civilization

The Fifth Golden Age was the Mayan civilization! As mentioned earlier, the Atlanteans, before the floods (which was described in the story of Noah's Ark), also fled to the Mayan civilization. Hence, you have the building of the great pyramids there as well. This, of course, was the Atlantean Masters building the Fifth Golden Age in South America, until it fell Spiritually back into a third-dimensional consciousness as did Egypt!

Sixth Golden Age: Ancient Greece

The Sixth Golden Age was Ancient Greece. We have all heard of the renaissance of civilization there for a period of time. Orpheus, Socrates, Plato, the Oracle of Delphi! This was the Sixth Golden Age on our planet!

Seventh Golden Age: Present Aquarian Age we are now moving into

The Seventh Golden Age is the new Aquarian Age we are now just on the edge of moving into. It is the New Age Movement around the world. It is the Renaissance of Religion and Spirituality around the world! At its core are the Teachings of the Ascended Masters and the Initiation and Ascension work that is exploding around the planet. It started with the Theosophical Movement began by Madam Blavatsky, which was the First Ascended Master Dispensation. Followed by the Second Ascended Master Dispensation of the Alice Bailey books as telepathically channeled by Djwhal Khul, and the Third Ascended Master Dispensation of *The "I Am" Discourses* of Saint Germain as channeled by Godfre Ray King. The Fourth Dispensation of Ascended Masters teachings is this 50-volume Ascension Book Series you are now reading! It is a movement of the synthesis and eclectic nature of God! It is a period of history now of the externalization of the Spiritual Hierarchy, which is the Spiritual Government of this planet! It should be noted here that one of the events that is about to take place is the incarnation on Earth of Jesus/Sananda in 2007, among just one of many Masters who are presently here and who will be materializing bodies. The Seventh Golden Age, however, will not be the worship of one Master, but will be the recognition that the Spiritual Christ/Buddha Consciousness lives within all beings and that all beings on Earth are, in truth, incarnations of God. This will be a period of history where the inner plane Ashrams of the inner plane Ascended Masters will be made manifest on the Earth! It will be a time of Initiation and the Path of Ascension being taught openly on Earth. It will be a time of the cleansing of the world's religions of the contamination of negative ego and the recognition that all paths lead to God. The one other great teaching of the Seventh Golden Age, which Spirit and the inner plane Ascended Masters are guiding me to speak of and close this chapter with, is the understanding that the emphasis of the Seventh Golden Age is not just on

Ascension, but on what has been called "Integrated Ascension"! The keynote and Revelation for the next millennium and Seventh Golden Age is for people, disciples, Initiates, and Masters alike, of all Spiritual paths, mystery schools, and religions, to become "Integrated Spiritual Masters"! This means that self-mastery and integration must be developed on a Spiritual, Psychological, and Physical/Earthly level in a balanced and integrated manner. This is the hallmark, touchstone, and thread of all the books you will read in this Spiritual Encyclopedia. It is the main thrust and emphasis of Spirit and the inner plane Ascended Masters' teachings and the main thrust of the Divine Plan for this Seventh Golden Age! This understanding and teaching is also the key to anchoring and activating your "Integrated Light Body"! This is not the period in Earth's history to just anchor the Light Body into the Spiritual Body and be disintegrated and fragmented on all other levels. This is the period of history or the first time on Earth where the thrust of the teachings is to develop an "Integrated Light Body"—Spiritually, Psychologically, Physically, and in all Four Faces Of GOD—Spiritual, Mental, Emotional, and Material! This is the new cutting-edge paradigm for this, the Seventh Golden Age on this planet!

3

The Five Dispensations of Ascended Master Teachings

My Beloved Readers, I am writing this chapter upon request of my dear friend Master El Morya, who thought it would be helpful to lightworkers to have an overview of the Ascended Master Teachings, Dispensations, and Organizations of the past, present, and future. Because of my great Love and respect for Master M, when he asked me to do this I was very happy to oblige and to make manifest on this Earthly plane this most wondrous legacy of Ascended Master Dispensations on the Earthly plane! There are five basic dispensations of Ascended Master teachings in our present age that have been and will be brought forth to this planet! This is not to say that a great many others have not greatly added and contributed to the knowledge brought forth to the present learning and understanding of Ascended Master Teachings. For especially in this present modern era, there has been a great many contributions in writings to the legacy of the Ascended Masters. These Dispensations I am speaking of here are a large series of Ascended Master Teachings books brought forth to lay the foundation for the Ascended Masters' work!

The First Dispensation was, of course, by the great Madam Blavatsky, now known on the inner plane as Lady Helena. She was, of course, the founder and main channel and scribe for Kuthumi, Saint Germain, El Morya, and the Ascended Masters for the first Dispensation of Ascended Master Teachings in the late 1800's and early 1900's. She wrote a voluminous amount of channeled material on the Ascended Masters. Madam Blavatsky was one of the greatest channels of our time. She founded the Theosophical Movement! She worked very closely with another wonderful teacher by the name of C.W. Leadbeater, who was also instrumental in later stages of the Theosophical Movement and who wrote some wonderful, easier to read books on the Ascended Master Teachings. One that stands out in my mind is a book called *The Masters and the Path*! Both Madam Blavatsky and Leadbeater worked very closely with Colonel Henry S. Olcott, who was kind of like Madam Blavatsky's right hand man and a great healer in his own right! Later, Annie Besant joined the group and took on much of the work of the Theosophical Movement. It was this organization, The Theosophical Movement, under the leadership of Madam Blavatsky and C.W. Leadbeater, that took on the assignment of finding a suitable candidate on the Earthly plane for Lord Maitreya, the Planetary Christ on the inner plane, to "Overlight" in a similar vein as he did for the Master Jesus 2000 years previously! Five candidates were selected; however, only one was chosen. This was Krishnamurti! Krishnamurti was a totally uneducated Indian boy who Madam Blavatasky and C.W. Leadbeater took under their wing, so to speak, and trained to become the next "Christed Vehicle" for the Earth. This training went on for a great many years and the Theosophical Movement developed a tremendous following around the world because of the collective efforts of these valiant souls who were really the groundbreakers of the first Ascended Master Dispensation! Madam Blavatsky was clearly the head of the organization and wrote, I believe, over 20 books that still, to this day, hold the testament of time.

Krishnamurti upon entering adulthood changed his mind, as did Lord Maitreya and the Spiritual Hierarchy, as to the original plan of Overlighting, and Krishnamurti left the Theosophical Movement and chose to cut himself off from the Ascended Masters, which was a long story in itself. He chose to follow his own path, which, of course, was his Divine Right, and continued his work until his passing in the not so distant past in the Ojai, California area! For those interested in learning more about Madam Blavatsky, C.W. Leadbeater, Colonel Henry Olcott, Krishnamurti, and Annie Besant, I would humbly recommend reading my book *The Ascended Masters Light The Way*! I have written four most wondrous chapters on the highlights of the life of Madam Blavatsky, C.W. Leadbeater, Colonel Henry Olcott, and Krishnamurti. This is indeed a most wondrous story of the First Dispensation of Ascended Master Teachings.

It is also very interesting to note that Madam Blavatsky had personal physical contact with the Ascended Masters Kuthumi, El Morya, and Djwhal Khul; who were all physically incarnated and at that time living in Tibet! I also believe she had physical contact with Saint Germain as well. Actual photographs were taken of them all together, which I believe many of you have seen! For those who have not read these four chapters in my book, I think you would find this first Dispensation of Ascended Master Teachings quite interesting reading! I would like to take this time to honor Madam Blavatsky (Lady Helena) and those great souls who helped to lay the First Dispensation of Ascended Master Teachings on the Earth!

The Second Dispensation of Ascended Master Teachings are the incredible books written by the Ascended Master Djwhal Khul! As you all know from reading my books, Djwhal Khul is a very dear friend and close mentor of mine! Djwhal Khul was the Master Kuthumi's main disciple, initiate, and friend at the time of the Theosophical Movement. He appeared physically to Madam Blavatsky on at least one occasion that I can remember for sure. Djwhal Khul in his past life was Confucius, the great Sage of China. He was also one of the Three Wise Men in the Story of Jesus, along with El Morya and Master Kuthumi! Saint Germain was

Joseph, the husband to Mother Mary! So, they all met up again 2000 years later to lay the very early initial foundation for the next 2000 year cycle! Quite interesting wouldn't you say, my Beloved Readers! I believe at the time of the Theosophical Movement even Lord Maitreya may have made some physical appearances, for El Morya, Kuthumi, Saint Germain, and Djwhal Khul were all very close and at least three of them were living in Tibet very close together. The Ascended Master Djwhal Khul was also in a past life Kleinias, a disciple of Pythagoras, who, of course, was Master Kuthumi in a past life. Master Kuthumi in past lives has also been Saint Francis, the architect of the Taj Mahal, John the Beloved, and a disciple of Jesus. El Morya was Balthazar of the Three Wise Men, I believe, with Kuthumi being Melchior and Djwhal Khul being Casper. El Morya was also Abraham, the founder of the Jewish religion, and Lord Maitreya was Krishna in a past life. Saint German was in his past lives Columbus, the Prophet Samuel in the Jewish religion, Francis Bacon (Shakespeare), and Merlin. So this is quite an interesting crew we have here!

Djwhal Khul telepathically channeled 22 volumes of Ascended Master Teachings through Alice Bailey who was also one of the greatest channels of our present day! It is to this day one of the most comprehensive dispensations of Ascended Master Teachings ever brought forth to the Earth! They stand as a tremendous Spiritual monument to the work of the Spiritual Hierarchy and Ascended Masters!

Djwhal Khul physically ascended in the late 1940's, which means in this case he turned his physical body into light and returned to the spiritual world! There, Master Kuthumi gave him Spiritual Leadership of the "Inner Plane Synthesis Ashram," which is a sub-ashram of the Second Ray Ashram of Master Kuthumi. This ashram is in charge of training all the disciples and initiates on the Earth in the area of Spiritual Education and Synthesis training in the Seven Rays. It is the only ashram on the inner plane that's specific purpose is the synthesis of all Seven Rays! The Second Ray is the Ray of Love/Wisdom and its focus is "Spiritual Education"! This is such a big job on Earth and that is why Lord Maitreya and Master

Kuthumi decided to create the Second Inner Plane Ashram. It is also because Master Kuthumi, who is the Chohan of the Second Ray, is training to take over the position of Planetary Christ when Lord Maitreya moves to his next Cosmic position! Master Kuthumi is so busy with this other work that he needed a trustworthy Master to train a great many of the Second Ray disciples and initiates and all disciples and initiates needing spiritual education and training in how to integrate all Seven Rays! Djwhal Khul has taken on a great many of Master Kuthumi's students so Master Kuthumi could focus on the cosmic work that he is involved in! Master Kuthumi and Djwhal Khul are extremely close friends, as is Master El Morya, Lord Maitreya, Saint Germain, and all the Ascended Masters!

On the inner plane, the Second Ray Ashram is a three story building complex of immense size and beauty! Djwhal Khul runs the first floor, known as the Inner Plane Synthesis Ashram! Master Kuthumi runs the second floor as the Chohan, or Lord, of that Ray, and Lord Maitreya, the Planetary Christ, runs the third floor! These are the three main Masters that run the Second Ray Department of Spiritual Education and the Love/Wisdom Ray for this planet! El Morya is the Chohan of the First Ray of Power, which focuses on the political arena on Earth! Serapis Bey is the Chohan for the Third Ray of Active Intelligence, which deals with the business side of Earth life! Paul the Venetian is Chohan for the Fourth Ray, which is Harmony, Beauty, and the Arts! His job is the harmonizing, beautification, and training in the spiritual side of the Arts! The Chohan for the Fifth Ray is Master Hilarion, with the focus on the Concrete Mind and New Age Science. The Sixth Ray Chohan is Sananda. This is also quite an interesting story, for Sananda in past lives was, of course, Jesus, Amilius, Adam, Melchizedek teacher of Abraham (El Morya), Enoch, Zend—the father of Zoroaster (Buddha), Ur, Asapha, Apollonius of Tynnia, Jeshua, and Joshua, who took over for Moses and led the Jewish people into the Promised Land. Isn't this interesting? The Seventh Ray is Lady Portia and Saint Germain in the area of Ceremonial Order and Magic, Freedom, Transmutation, Alchemy, the Violet Flame, and the

Restructuring, Organization and Grounding of the Divine Plan on Earth! Allah Gobi is the Manu of the First Ray. Lord Maitreya is the Planetary Christ, as I said. Saint German is also serving now as the Mahachohan! Lord Buddha has taken over the position of Planetary Logos, or President of the Planet, from Sanat Kumara who has moved to his next higher Cosmic position and is overlighting Lord Buddha in his work! Lord Buddha in past lives was, of course, Orpheus, the great Greek Master. He was Arjuna, disciple of Krishna (Lord Maitreya). He was Thoth/Hermes, the great Egyptian Master, builder of the Pyramids and the author of the Great Hermetic Laws; Vyassa, the Scribe for the *Bhagavad-Gita*; and Zoroaster, the Great Persian Spiritual Master!

So my Beloved Readers, I think you can see that, in truth, this story of the Ascended Masters really began much earlier than this First Dispensation of Ascended Master Teachings with Madam Blavatsky and the Theosophical Movement. It has its first antecedents in all the religions of the Earth!

My Beloved Readers, I have a few more things I wish to say about Djwhal Khul and Alice Bailey; however, before I do this I want to share the Third Dispensation of Ascended Master Teachings, which are *The "I Am" Discourses* channeled by Godfre Ray King. This is also, my Beloved Readers, a most interesting story, for Godfre Ray King in his past life was none other than George Washington, the first President of the United States! Is it not fitting that he would be the channel to bring forth *The "I Am" Discourses* for Saint Germain to the United States and the world? This was another 18-volume series of books that, I believe, brought forth another fantastic Dispensation of Ascended Master Teachings to the planet. Beloved Saint Germain brought forth the most wondrous teachings of the "The Mighty I Am Presence"! These are most wonderful books! Very easy to read and to bring forth the Science of Invocation and Affirmation using the "I Am" as only Saint Germain can! These books blend very nicely with the 22 volumes written by Alice Bailey and Djwhal Khul!

As the story goes, Saint German physically materialized to Godfre Ray King in the 1930's, which began a whole story and series of books channeled by Saint Germain and other Ascended Masters! Godfre Ray King is another one of the great channels of our time! Saint Germain has made a wonderful contribution to this planet again as he has in the past in bringing forth these teachings!

In addition, around this time it is noteworthy to say, not in the sense of a Dispensation, but as a very great contribution to the collected work of Ascended Master Teachings, that Master El Morya, through Nicolas Roerich, brought forth another series of books on Agni Yoga. I believe there were around 15 or 16 books in this series, which was another catalyst to the legacy of the Ascended Masters' Dispensations!

Also, in this vein of noteworthy contributions by the Ascended Masters is the set of books written in the 1970's by the Master Jesus, known as *A Course in Miracles*. The Master Jesus took on the Spiritual Assignment as only he could do, of explaining the difference between Christ thinking and egotistical thinking in this three-volume set—Textbook, Lesson book, and Teacher's Manual! Truly one of the most incredible set of books and Divine Revelations of Ascended Master Teachings of our time! Jesus channeled these books through a Jewish woman, who when asked why she was chosen for this assignment the Master Jesus said, "…because she would do it and would not put a lot of her own interpretations and opinions into the work"! She indeed did as Jesus requested!

One other noteworthy contribution is Djwhal Khul returning in the 1970's with Vywamus, the Higher Aspect of Sanat Kumara, to found the Tibetan Foundation. This was done through the channeling work and books of Janet McLure! I believe she passed on in the late 70's or early 80's, but brought forth some wonderful channelings from Djwhal Khul and Vywamus to continue this Ascended Mastery legacy. The Tibetan Foundation is no longer in operation; however, I would like to take this time to honor Janet McLure for her wonderful contribution to this legacy!

Djwhal Khul in the 1940's, after "Physically Ascending" and turning his body to light, continued to telepathically communicate with Alice Bailey from the inner planes. Before that, he was living in Tibet and was telepathically channeling the books from there to Alice Bailey. I would also at this time like to honor Alice Bailey and Djwhal Khul for the wonderful contribution they both have made through these writings to this Ascended Mastery legacy!

To continue this most interesting story of the Ascended Mastery Dispensations, organizations, writings and legacy; Djwhal Khul in 1996 graciously asked me if I would consider taking over his "Inner Plane Synthesis Ashram" in the not too distant future, for he was preparing to get ready to leave for his next Cosmic position! At the time of his making this request I had published my first five books: *The Complete Ascension Manual, Soul Psychology, Beyond Ascension, Hidden Mysteries*, and *The Ascended Masters Light the Way*! I had also just completed my first Wesak Celebration in Mt. Shasta! I had been working very closely with him for many years and he had helped me, along with other Ascended Masters, to write many of my books. I was extremely well-versed and well-studied in all the previous Dispensations and contributions of Ascended Master Teachings. I had been a Spiritual Teacher, Spiritual Psychologist, and Channel for many years for the Masters, and had always felt an enormous attunement and kinship with the Ascended Masters' lineage and teachings! I was greatly honored by Djwhal Khul's and the Spiritual Hierarchy's invitation to take on this Spiritual Leadership assignment. The idea of being able to run the first floor of this inner plane ashram with Master Kuthumi and Lord Maitreya was most intriguing! Since 1996, I have been in training with Djwhal Khul, Melchizedek, the Mahatma, Archangel Metatron, and the Core Group of Masters I work with in preparation to take over this "Inner Plane Synthesis Ashram"! In the meantime, I was guided at that time to open the Melchizedek Synthesis Light Academy! This was the anchoring on Earth of the Inner Plane Synthesis Ashram overlighted by Djwhal Khul, Melchizedek, the Mahatma, Archangel

Metatron, and the Planetary Hierarchy I have mentioned in this chapter, and others such as the Divine Mother, Mother Mary, Quan Yin, Isis, Helios and Vesta, the Lord of Arcturus, the Lord of Sirius, the Ashtar Command, Sai Baba, and others. It has grown over the years and I humbly and lovingly call them all "Core Group"!

Anyway, to continue this story, I had already started writing, as I previously mentioned, my "Easy-to-Read Encyclopedia of the Spiritual Path"! I have currently completed over 42 volumes in this series of books. They are based upon the Ascended Master Teachings of the past, present, and future! They are both co-creative writings of my own and the Ascended Masters, creating a "Synthesis of all Ascended Master Teachings, Religions, Spiritual Paths, Mystery Schools, Sacred Writings, Spiritual Texts, Spiritual Teachers, and Gurus"! It has its foundation, however, in the writing of the Ascended Masters! However, because of my humble unique gift in the area of "Synthesis," I have tied the Ascended Master Teachings in with this synthesis effort to show the unification of all teachings! In truth, all teachings have their origin in the Universal Logos Melchizedek and what has been called the "Ancient and Sacred Order of Melchizedek"! In truth, we are all connected with this sacred order for we all live, move and have our being in the "The Melchizedek Universe" of which Melchizedek is the head. The name "Melchizedek" is one a great many people have called themselves or named themselves! Just because someone names himself or herself "Melchizedek," does not make them one. A "Melchizedek" in Ancient Teachings is considered a Seventh Degree Initiate! It is a Priest- and Priestess-hood! This is why a great many people on our Earth have taken on this name or are taking on this name, which is fine and beautiful! The Melchizedek I am speaking of here is Melchizedek, the Universal Logos and President of our entire Universe! So all of us, my Brothers and Sisters, are part of his Sacred Order!

I have plans to complete 100 volumes in my book series, and then this book series will be complete and I will have completed my Spiritual Assignment and mission in this specific regard! The unique things about these books are the comprehensiveness and scope of the work and how easy to read and practical they are. How they synthesize all that I have spoken of. How they address not just Spiritual Mastery, but all Psychological Mastery and Physical/Earthly Mastery, and how to integrate the three! Also, they bring forth from the Ascended Masters, I humbly suggest, some of the most cutting-edge Ascended Master Teachings in the area of Ascension, Spirituality, Psychology, Earthly Mastery and Healing ever brought forth! Djwhal Khul told me many years ago that this 100 volume series of books, of which I have completed 42 volumes, is the "Fourth Dispensation of Ascended Master Teachings" that he prophesied would come at the turn of the century and which he wrote about in the Alice Bailey books in the 1940's! I am very humbled and honored to have taken on this assignment, and to have been offered the position of taking over the "Inner Plane Synthesis Ashram" when Djwhal Khul moves on to his next Cosmic position. At this time I am very much enjoying anchoring the Synthesis Ashram and Academy on Earth under the guidance of Djwhal Khul, Melchizedek, the Mahatma, and the Core Group of inner plane Ascended Masters! When my mission on Earth is complete, I will take over this aforementioned Spiritual Assignment for which I am receiving great training and practice here on Earth! I feel an incredible love and connection with the Ascended Masters. They feel like my home, so to speak! I am greatly honored and humbled to be a link in this chain of Ascended Masters Teachings, Dispensations, and Legacy! It is my great hope and prayer that this current 42 volume series of books will bring forth the profound wonderment and enlightenment of this most rich Ascended Master tradition in a past, present and cutting-edge future sense on all levels!

My Beloved Readers, this now brings me to the Fifth and final Ascended Master Dispensation! This one is the future one that has not yet come to pass! It has been my job to lay the foundation and revelation for the New Millennium. It is my great honor, under the guidance and direction of the inner plane Ascended Masters, at this time to give a "bird's eye view" of what we are now preparing for in terms of the next Ascended Master Dispensation upon entering this New Millennium. Writing about this is one of the most enjoyable Spiritual Assignments I have ever taken on, for it truly is the Spiritual Vision of the Seventh Golden Age! On this note, I will begin!

My Beloved Readers, in the not too distant future a great change and transformation will be taking place on this planet, which, in truth, has already just begun. The previously hidden esoteric and hidden Mystery School Training will be made Exoteric! The Externalization of the Spiritual Hierarchy will be made fully manifest on the Earth! The "Houses and Temples of Light" will be reopened! Instead of the Pyramids being monoliths of past spiritual greatness, they and many other edifices of a like nature will be reopened to the greatness of their past! The inner plane ashrams of the Christ will be made manifest on the Earth. The Melchizedek Synthesis Light Academy and Ashram is one of the first of these to be made manifest! It has been my Spiritual Assignment and those of my fellow Masters and High Level Initiates and many others of you all over the world, to lay the groundwork and foundation for this to take place! Those members of the Spiritual Hierarchy on Earth will fully claim their rightful positions. The Seven Ashrams of the Christ will be fully anchored and headed by Masters and High Level Initiates on Earth. Actual initiations will be performed on Earth as they are on the Spiritual Plane! The traditions and secrets of the Mystery Schools will no longer be hidden! There will be open instruction and teaching. The inner mysteries will be totally revealed! The full Externalization of the Hierarchy will not just manifest in the area of Spiritual Education, but in all aspects of society. Masters and High Level Initiates will openly claim their positions in Politics, Government, Business, Economics, the Arts, Music, Architecture, all the New Age Sciences, Religion, and the complete reorganization and restructuring of society! Our educational system will be completely reformed and the Soul and Spirit will be reintroduced in a universal and synthesis manner that honors and is inclusive of all religions and alienates no one! Our prison systems will be reformed along spiritual principles. Violence and lust will be removed from our movies and media, for the people won't stand for it! Our legal system will be transformed. Partisan politics will be a thing of the past and a new form of civility, honor, and Spiritual/Christ/Buddha Consciousness will re-enter this most noble profession.

The veil between the inner plane Ascended Masters and the outer plane Externalization of the Hierarchy will be lifted! The Spiritual Government on the inner plane through its externalized Masters on Earth will begin to governmentally and politically lead the nations of the Earth!

The United Nations will be revamped to truly reflect all countries on the Earth! We will truly have a confederation of nations on Earth all working together under the Spiritual Leadership of the Ascended Masters and Spiritual inner plane government! This will lead to the admission by all governments of the existence of Extraterrestrials! This will lead to the open entering, en masse, of Christed Extraterrestrials to the Earth! This will cause an acceleration on our planet, the likes of which it has never known! They will help us rid our planet of pollution! They will help us get rid of all illness and disease! They will help us rebuild the "Houses and Temples of Light"! The Ancient Temples of Atlantis and Lemuria in their golden past ages will re-emerge! The Ancient Order of Melchizedek will be made manifest on Earth! The Extraterrestrials in conjunction with the inner plane Ascended Masters will bring new technologies and ideas to every aspect of our society. These are civilizations on other planets that have solved these issues and lessons hundreds and thousands of years ago! As we show ourselves responsible and prepared, more and more will be given! Every aspect of Society and Civilization will be reorganized and re-formed under the Divine Plan of the inner plane Ascended Masters, under the Divine Plan of Lord Buddha, Lord Maitreya, the Manu Allah Gobi, the Mahachohan and the Seven Chohans, Saint Germain, Djwhal Khul and the Synthesis Ashram! There will be much more open and direct contact and much clearer communication between the inner plane Ashrams,

Masters, Initiates, and Government and Political Leaders! We will begin to slowly but surely return to how it was in Lemuria before the fall and densification of matter occurred! Matter is now in the process of slowly but surely becoming more etheric in nature as it was in the beginning! The next 1000 years will continue this process until eventually we will return to a place where it was in the beginning, in the Garden of Eden of Lemuria! We are the Light Bearers for a New Age! Sai Baba will reincarnate again for his third incarnation in his triple avatar incarnation! The Archangels and Angels will also be part of this New Revelation! They will be more openly honored, revered, and accepted as the noble Servants of GOD that they are. They will reveal themselves much more openly and their mysteries and teachings will be unfolded! The Elohim line of evolution will be added to this mix as well! There will be an integrated working together of the inner plane Ascended Masters, Archangels and Angels, Elohim Councils, Christed Extraterrestrials, and Masters and Initiates on Earth! Adding to this mix will be the complete returning of the Divine Mother and the Goddess energies to Earth. The Goddess energies have been abused and banished from the Earth for eons of time! This will completely change! Total equality will reign! Women will be paid as much as men! Women will take over governmental and political positions! The end of the Patriarchy will have come! All prejudice and racism will be removed from our society! The Divine Mother and the Goddess energies will finally be given their proper honor and reverence! Brotherhoods and Sisterhoods of Light will reign supreme! The Goddess path will be revered as highly as the God path! The Goddess will take over more and more positions in the Spiritual Government as well! In truth, they already have, they are just not known about!

As part of this process, Mother Earth will finally be honored as the living, Sacred Being she is! Honoring and sanctifying the Earth will be one of our biggest priorities. The Earth will be removed of all pollution and returned to her pristine Edenic State! There will also be much greater honoring of the Animal, Plant, and Mineral Kingdoms! They will be seen as our younger Brothers and Sisters and will be seen as the incarnations of God that they are!

Part of this transformation will also see the honoring of the Nature Kingdom, Pan, the Nature Spirits, Plant Devas and Elementals! There will be an open communication between the people of the Earth and these etheric beings that control all of nature! They will again fully return to Earth and all Her gardens and farms!

There will be the open communication of all these different beings I have mentioned in this chapter under the guidance of the inner plane Ascended Masters! Lord Buddha holds the Divine Plan for our planet, which he receives from Helios and Vesta, which they receive from Melchior, which he receives from Melchizedek, which he receives from GOD, Christ, and the Holy Spirit! It is stepped down at each level so the entire Universe unfolds according to GOD's Plan! Lord Buddha will give the Divine Plan to the Manu, the Christ, and the Mahachohan, as well as the Seven Chohans, Djwhal Khul and the Synthesis Ashram. They will then disseminate this Divine Plan to all Masters and Higher Level Initiates on Earth in all aspects of Earth life! Each of the Seven Ashrams of the Christ and the Synthesis Ashram will be in charge of a different aspect of the Divine Plan to Manifest on Earth, both in a Heavenly and Earthly sense!

The Religions of the world will also be revamped to free them from the contamination of negative ego programming and dogma. As negative ego is cleared from the religions, they will become much more united and inclusive in nature, and all competition and self-righteousness will end! They will also be seen as pathways to GOD that are equally valued! There will always be different religions and this is good! However, they will cooperate much more in the future under the Spiritual Leadership of the Ascended Masters!

As time progresses, the governments and political leaders of our world will be Spiritual Masters and High Level Initiates! The Ascended Masters will have led us to build a new Utopian civilization! It will be a Fifth-Dimensional civilization, not a third-dimensional civilization! One of the blueprints the inner plane Ascended Masters will use is the blueprint of the Arcturian civilization! Arcturus is the most advanced civilization in our galaxy. They are approximately 3000 years ahead of us! They will bring their Technologies and Spiritual Wisdom, in conjunction with the Ascended Masters, to help us more quickly solve all the great pressing issues of our times! The rainforests will be saved! The ozone layer repaired! All pollution will be removed! Pesticide use stopped! New forms of energy, based on principles like those that Nikola Tesla brought to the planet, will come, and we will no longer burn fossil fuels for energy! Free forms of energy will be created! With free forms of energy, all pollution will end! Control of our worlds by Power Elite and Secret Governments will end! Abuse of all kinds will end! All war will end! The Earth will join its rightful conscious place in the Confederation of Planets of our Solar System, Galaxy, and Universe. With the help of Extraterrestrial technology, space travel to other worlds will actually be a possibility!

There will be open Spiritual, Scientific, and Technological exchange! All Spiritual Paths, Mystery Schools, and Spiritual Traditions will be honored under the rulership of Ascended Masters! Great Spiritual Masters from the inner plane will incarnate on Earth! Lord Maitreya may incarnate again in 700 years as the new Cosmic Christ!

With the society totally changed under the direct leadership of the Ascended Masters, it will not be such a major decision for inner plane Ascended Masters to choose to come to Earth as it is now!

So, in conclusion, this Fifth Dispensation of Ascended Master Teachings and Organization will be a most glorious one! My Beloved Readers, we are not that far away, I am happy to see, and yet there is much work to be done! It is all of our jobs, as the Light Bearers for the New Age, to lay the foundation and groundwork for all of this to take place! We are living on the brink of one of the most glorious times in the history of this Earth! We are literally on the brink of the Realization of the Seventh Golden Age on this planet! It is my sincere hope and prayer that you have enjoyed the Masters and my sharing of rich Spiritual Tradition, Legacy,

Present Condition, and Future Dispensation of the Ascended Masters on Earth! It has been my great honor and joy to share this past, present, and future Story of the Ascended Masters on Earth with you.

4

Understanding the Nature of God Consciousness, Soul Retrieval and Soul Fragments

In one of my conversations with the Mahatma I asked about soul retrieval and soul fragments, which is an issue that I have always been interested in, being a Spiritual Psychologist as part of my mission. I have written extensively in my book *The Complete Ascension Manual* about how everyone has an Oversoul, or Higher Self, that is in charge of 12 Souls that incarnate in different worlds to gain love, wisdom, power and virtue for the development of the Oversoul. Each person also has 12 Oversouls, which make up the Monad, or Mighty I Am Presence. This means that each person is made up of 144 Souls in the Monadic, or Mighty I Am Presence, family soul, so to speak.

I have also written extensively in my book *Cosmic Ascension* about the importance of integrating and cleansing Soul Extensions or Souls, not only from one's Oversoul and Monad, but also from one's Monadic Group connections. In other words, as one evolves beyond the Monad, one forms group consciousness networks or modules. It is also possible to integrate and cleanse soul extensions from these Monadic Modules, hypothetically all the way back to Source! This is one of the many keys to accelerating evolution!

It must be understood that the nature of God is consciousness. God is, in a sense, the Omniversal Soul! If you think about what Creation is, it is God just splitting His omniversal consciousness into forms. God breathes them up or Big Bangs them out in one mighty conscious breath in a Day of Brahma, and then breathes them back in. A Cosmic Day and a Cosmic Night. God takes smaller breaths for each universe and one bigger breath for all universes. God creates the Cosmic Monads, which might also be called "God Cells"! Each of these 12 God Cells, or Cosmic Monads, contain infinite numbers of Monads, or Mighty I Am Presences, as we know them. Then these Monads, or Mighty I Am Presences, go out into Creation and each creates 12 Oversouls, and/or Higher Selves. Each of these Oversouls, and/or Higher Selves, then go out and create 12 Souls, which is what we are. We are each one soul who has incarnated from our Oversoul. So you see, my friends, God splits His consciousness to create the God Cell, or Cosmic Monad, which splits its consciousness to create the infinite numbers of individualized Monads, which splits its consciousness to each create 12 Oversouls, which splits its consciousness to create 12 Souls, which incarnate on different planets and different dimensions to evolve the Oversoul, which is evolving the Monad, or Mighty I Am Presence, which is evolving the Group Modules of Monads, which is evolving the Cosmic Monad, or God Cells, which are evolving to Ascend God!

Now everyone is focusing on their individual Ascension, which is fine and appropriate, however, from a Group Consciousness lens, which can also be looked at simultaneously, there is only one Ascension and that is God Ascension! We are all the Eternal Self, or incarnations of God, or Aspects of God's Consciousness being breathed back to God. It is all God's play. There are no separate individuals. We are all just different kinds of flowers in the Garden of God. There are three lineages of flowers, however, which are: Ascended Master, Angelic, and Elohim. However, at the end, even they all become one! There are different races of Extraterrestrial beings, like the Adam Kadmon form, the Grays, the Insect-looking ones, the Lizard races, the Cat race, the list is infinite, but these are all just different incarnations of God and/or different flowers of God in the Garden of God! Do you see, my beloved readers, it is just God splitting His consciousness into infinite forms. We are all Gods, serving other Gods, returning back to GOD the Creator! Do you see how silly war is, or competition, jealousy, or selfishness, for there are no beings but God. People get caught up the form of things and do not see the essence behind all forms. Flowers do not compete. Daisies do not fight with Roses or Lilies! It is just all God's Play and Drama. The Divine Plan and unique thing about our return home is that GOD wants his incarnations of Self to return home "Conscious"! In other words, to return home to our true identity in GOD, out of our free choice, not because He forces us to! So, do you see, my friends, that all Creation is just the splitting of God's Consciousness down the evolutionary ladder! This is just the hierarchical structure of things that is done so each level, in a sense, has a personal teacher to help them back up through the 352 levels back to GOD!

This is why Unconditional Love is so important, for it is all GOD! This is why sharing is so important, for it is all GOD! This is why seeing beyond appearances and form is so important while still being able to live in form and master form! This is why integration and balance is so important to learn at each level as we move up the evolutionary dimensional ladder of Consciousness. My Beloved Readers, you have been given a Spiritual vision here of Creation from the Full Spectrum Prism Lens of God! Where we focus on evolving our selves, God is focusing on evolving Universes. Where we are working with ourselves, our students and our planet to become Integrated Spiritual Masters; GOD is the Supreme Integrated Spiritual Master in charge of bringing all Creation into balance and integration within his Supreme Cosmic Body! The Elohim, the Cosmic and Planetary Ascended Masters, the Archangels and Angels, and Christed

Extraterrestrials are his agents throughout His Omniverse to help create this change. We are his agents on Earth at this time to create this change.

Once we achieve Christ Realization on a Planetary Level, we work on being Solar Christs. Then Galactic Christs! Then Universal Christs! Then Multiuniversal Christs! Then Cosmic Christs! There is no skipping levels. One must serve at each level and at each level of Initiation and master and integrate that level before being allowed to move up to the next! There are 352 levels of Initiation, and, hence, 352 levels of Light Body to anchor and integrate! There are 352 levels of consciousness to master! Each of these 352 levels are also connected to a chakra system that must be anchored, activated and actualized! GOD's Personality is made up of the 12 Great Cosmic Rays. Hence, we on Earth must learn to balance our Seven Rays on Earth and ultimately our Cosmic Rays, as well as everything else! Oneness and integration cannot be separated, for ultimately they are one in the same thing! Mastery, integration, and balance must be achieved at each level before one is allowed by the Grace of God and the Masters to move to the next! One must fully embody each level, demonstrate each level, and serve at each level before being allowed to move to the next! Each level one achieves is an initiation or ascension of sorts to the next level. The key is that it must not only be done in your Spiritual body, it also must be "integrated" into your mental, emotional, etheric, physical, and Earthly self and vehicle as well, as long as one has a physical/Earthly aspect to work with and through!

The Mahatma is a group consciousness being that embodies all 352 levels! This is why I specifically asked him about soul retrieval and soul fragments, which I have not really even explained yet. First, I had to lay the groundwork for this discussion, which I have just done by God and the Mahatma's grace!

Now in terms of soul retrieval and soul fragments, what the Mahatma told me is that in life as we connect with other people we create cords and threads and leave aspects of our energy with other people. This is a good thing and a gift from one God to another God, in a sense. Sometimes, however, there are certain energy pieces that it may be Spiritually appropriate to draw back to one's soul. These are called "soul fragments." This is not something you have to figure out consciously yourself, you can just ask God, the Mahatma, Melchizedek, Metatron and Archangel Michael to do for you. The basic request should be to return to you all soul fragments that are Spiritually appropriate to return and to leave the ones as Spiritual gifts that are pieces of energy that are meant to stay with all the people you have loved and touched in some way! Very simple to do, but very important to set up and request!

In a similar vein, I would also recommend calling in Archangel Michael and Faith, and request that all energy cords and lines of energy from this life, all past lives, and all inner plane connections between lives since your creation, be cut that are not Spiritually appropriate. Again, this is not something you have to consciously figure out, it can just be requested and, by the Grace of Archangel Michael and Faith, can be done in an instant! Simple but profound! Is this not the nature of God?

It is my humble hope and prayer that this chapter has given you a Spiritual vision and glimpse into understanding from GOD"s perspective the nature of Consciousness, Souls, Soul Retrieval, and Soul Fragments. It has been my great joy and pleasure to channel and write this chapter as well!

Kodoish, Kodoish, Kodoish Adonai Tsabayoth!

Holy, Holy, Holy is the Lord God of Hosts!

5

A Cosmic Day and a Cosmic Night

Those who have read my books know that a Cosmic Day lasts for 4.3 billion years. Then there is the Cosmic Night, which lasts for a similar amount of time. This has been termed the "in-breath" and "out-breath" of Brahma. We on Earth have used up 3.1 billion years of our Cosmic Day and therefore have 1.2 billion years before our Cosmic Night begins. I have always been interested in what goes on during the Cosmic Night, so I put on my Sherlock Holmes hat and attempted to pin the Masters down on this point.

During the Cosmic Night, there is a kind of incubation period before Brahma, or God, takes His next out-breath. In a Cosmic Night, the physical planets do not evolve but souls who are now out of incarnation do still evolve. Melchizedek said that incarnations, in a sense, continue not on the physical plane but rather on the astral plane, which was a total surprise and new concept to me, yet it made total sense.

The physical planets go into hibernation. There also seems to be a speeding up on the inner plane because of the lack of resistance that is brought about because of the fact that material existence does not have to be dealt with at this time. Souls continue to reincarnate on the astral plane until they break the wheel of reincarnation and transcend the physical laws. This is the attaining of the seventh initiation.

Melchizedek said that whatever kind of role the given soul was playing in the physical, that soul plays the opposite in the astral plane, just like the contrast of day and night. This allows for balanced growth and the proper integration of all archetypes.

An example of this might be someone who has been very intent on making money as his/her main focus and was very wealthy and miserly. In the Cosmic Night, the person would incarnate on an astral plane where he would be very poor in terms of monetary wealth and hence would be forced to learn how to grow spiritually without this attachment. The Cosmic Night also allows each soul an enormously long period of time to think, introspect, and digest its hundreds of lifetimes in material existence and the many thousands of lifetimes of its oversoul, which is made of each person's eleven other soul extensions.

Each soul extension usually has from 200 to 250 incarnations. This is similar to the time each of us has had between our incarnations during a Cosmic Day. This is really the break time between incarnations for an incarnation of an entire universe. You must realize here that we are only talking about one Cosmic Day. Think of how long a year of Brahma is, or one hundred years of Brahma, which is the period of one solar system. I have enclosed a chart from *The Complete Ascension Manual* that deals with this timeline and that is originally from the Alice Bailey material. God's infinite universes are made up of infinite numbers of these occult or cosmic centuries, which is a concept that cannot even be fathomed by the linear mind.

One hundred years of Brahma	An occult century; the period of a solar system
One year of Brahma	The period of seven chains, where the seven planetary schemes are concerned
One week of Brahma	The period of seven rounds in one scheme; it has a chain significance
One day of Brahma	The occult period of a round
One hour of Brahma	Concerns interchain affairs
One Brahmic minute	Concerns the planetary centers and therefore egoic groups
One Brahmic moment	Concerns an egoic group and its relation to the whole

As an evolving being we receive the whole balance of cosmic experience by moving in and out of these Cosmic Days and Cosmic Nights every 4.3 billion years. On a microcosmic level we do this every Earth day. Every twenty-four hour Earth day we have a microcosmic day (waking hours) and a microcosmic night (sleep time). Did not Hermes/Thoth say, "As within, so without. As above, so below"? Understand the atom and you can understand the infinite universe. Know thyself, and hence you can know God.

Once one incarnates into a particular universe (and there are infinite numbers of universes, each with a different cosmic theme), one does not leave that universe until he/she graduates, which would mean becoming a full-fledged Melchizedek, not in the Earthly sense of the term, but in the highest universal sense of the term, as a Sai Baba, for example. He is the only being in incarnation even close to operating at that level.

So, there might be what is called a planetary Melchizedek, a solar Melchizedek, a galactic Melchizedek (Lord Maitreya), and a universal Melchizedek (Sai Baba). There is one level after this, the multi-universal level Melchizedek, which would be full and complete graduation from the Melchizedek school. The next step after this is Source, or God, merger. This is the step that Melchizedek, our Universal Logos, who runs the universe, is now moving toward. So even *he* is in a state of evolution, as is Sai Baba.

Part of the work of the Cosmic Night is to prepare oneself and to do all the work to prepare for one's next evolution in the Cosmic Day. This is the same principle as the time between incarnations. Most souls do not incarnate immediately after passing on. A rest period is needed, and time for introspection and review.

The same principle is in operation on the universal level, a period of activity and non-activity, in a material sense. In a psychic or spiritual sense, just like our inner plane dreamtime, it is still very active. If you realized how much you do every night while you are asleep, you would be amazed. Most of us remember only one-tenth of one percent of all the spiritual work and service work we are involved in. On the psychic or spiritual level this never stops.

Melchizedek and Djwhal Khul told me that in the original design of the Cosmic Day it was thought that souls would only do physical evolving and not astral incarnations. It was found, however, that this was much too taxing on the mental body. Because of this the process of astral incarnations was instituted so the mental body could rest from the taxing process of creating physical form. The Masters said that the Cosmic Night is speeded up in some mysterious way because of the nonmaterial existence, so, in truth, it isn't as long as a Cosmic Day.

This process of astral incarnations reminds me of what has taken place during the initiations in the Great Pyramid of Giza in the King's Chamber while lying in the sarcophagus. Souls were allowed to accelerate evolution by living out incarnations in the dream state in the Great Pyramid to achieve the process of becoming a planetary Melchizedek in a shorter period of time (*Hidden Mysteries* details this in chapters on the Egyptian mysteries).

During a Cosmic Night the physical universe still exists, but is in a state of suspended animation waiting for the incarnation cycle to begin again. The Masters then chimed in with another amazing piece of information that they said was a side note to this whole line of questioning. They said that the key to our learning dematerialization and materialization lay within this understanding of the Cosmic Day and Cosmic Night.

The next piece of information transported us into the Twilight Zone, and you will see what I mean when you read this. To be honest, it is hard for me to believe that this is true. I think I once saw an actual *Twilight Zone* TV episode using a similar theme (you probably saw this one too). If this came through accurately, what they said is that when the Cosmic Night actually begins the six billion people living on our planet don't physically instantly die and neither do the beings on the ten billion other planets with life in the universe.

I asked, "If they don't physically die, what happens to them?" The Masters said they are held in suspended animation with the rest of the universe and the essence, or souls, in incarnation live on. At the exact moment of the beginning of the Cosmic Day 4.3 billion years later (no real time on the inner: it is a concept of material existence), everything begins exactly where things left off with everyone in the universe back in incarnation exactly the way they were before they left, except 4.3 billion years wiser.

Is that a trip or is that a trip! Do you remember the *Twilight Zone* episode where the man somehow obtained a pocket watch that could stop time for everyone on Earth except for himself? Everyone else was frozen in time, but he could move around. I can't remember how it ended, but I think at first he liked it and then he began to hate it, and then at the end I think he dropped the watch and it cracked and broke and he was stuck in the Cosmic Night.

I remember reading something in a metaphysical book that for some reason has always stuck in my mind and I had never asked the Masters if it was true or not. What was written was that if a person who was still involved in the reincarnation cycle died in the month of December as a Sagittarius, then he/she would be reborn their next life as a Sagittarius according to Cosmic Law.

This concept of suspended animation and picking up exactly where one left off 4.3 billion years earlier reminded me of this. I don't know if this theory is true; I will have to check this out the next time I meditate. It sure is an interesting thought, however, and does make sense. As Edgar Cayce said in regard to the Law of Karma, "Every jot and tittle of the law is fulfilled." What you sow, you reap. And what you put out comes back to you. No one gets something for nothing. The Masters call this a "stopaction frame."

If you think about this, it is exactly what goes on every night when we go to sleep. The physical body is held in a state of suspended animation and the etheric, astral, mental, buddhic, atmic, monadic, logoic, and soul bodies are off to their different planes of existence. When we wake up in the morning we continue exactly where we left off, one planetary night wiser. In a cosmic sense, it is like going to sleep for a Cosmic Night, instead of just a planetary night. You have to admit, it makes a lot of sense: Whenever there is the correlation between the microcosm and the macrocosm, there is always a ring of truth. This would make a great storyline for a *Star Trek* movie, wouldn't you agree?

The Masters continued with their discussion telling me that this could be equated to time travel. Look at when we dream, it feels like hours and days go by and in true chronological time it has been only seconds. This process is the exact reverse: Eons of time go by and from the perspective of the physical body it has not even been a second. This is possible because we are dealing with non-time and space realities. Time is a linear concept created by the third-dimensional mind. It is multi-dimensional and simultaneous in the spiritual world.

I then asked, "When does a universe achieve its ascension?" The universe achieves its ascension when all the souls incarnated in the entire universe achieve cosmic ascension in their given universal school. Our universal school is the Melchizedek school. Other universes have different cosmic themes (as I talk about in *Beyond Ascension)*.

The theme for our Cosmic Day in the Melchizedek school or university is "Courage." Other universes, of which there are infinite numbers, each have a different Universal Logos, hence a different school and a different cosmic theme. A very interesting side note here is that Vywamus, in one of his channelings through Janet McClure, said that the Extraterrestrials called the Grays, who are connected with Zeta Reticuli, are very sick physically and are affected this way because they traveled in spaceships from a different universe. He said they will never recover on their own without cosmic spiritual help, for they weren't created to evolve through this universe. I personally find this absolutely fascinating.

When all beings graduate from Melchizedek's cosmic school, Melchizedek said that the universe dissolves into light and the next universe is created. Metatron refers to this in *The Book of Knowledge: The Keys of Enoch* when he speaks of the possibility of receiving the information from the next universe and the pyramid grid from the next universe. Just as Arcturus is the future self, or prototype, for planet Earth, being the most evolved civilization in our galaxy, so planets, solar systems, galaxies, universes, and multi-universes are all in a state of evolution and ascension as well as ourselves.

In the Alice Bailey books Djwhal Khul spoke of the Jewish race being the most evolved race from the previous, or third solar system. We are now in the fourth solar system. This ties in to the understanding that was brought forth in the Alice Bailey books and in the Theosophical books of Madam Blavatsky of an occult period of a round, involving seven rounds that make up one scheme and seven schemes that make up one occult century.

On our planet this is divided on a more microcosmic level into the seven root races. Each root race is connected to the evolution of one planetary chakra. The universe is as ordered and mathematical in its evolution as a Swiss-made watch. Everything in God's universe is governed by laws, including God. To get even a glimpse of this process puts one into a state of absolute awesome amazement.

After a universe's completion, graduation, and ascension, there is a new universe created with a new and more evolved cosmic theme.

Just as the lightworkers on this planet and others like it will eventually fill those posts. The Galactic Masters will ultimately evolve to fill the posts in the universal level of government. The Universal Masters such as Melchizedek will ultimately move on to the multi-universal level and beyond back to Source to fill cosmic posts in the ultimate cosmic government.

This is the cosmic hierarchy of Creation and a vision of our cosmic journey. Can you imagine being in charge of an entire universe? It is sometimes hard enough just being in charge of a physical, emotional and mental body. This is why we have to master each level of school—planetary, solar, galactic, universal, multi-universal and cosmic, step by step. It is a long journey, but again, what is the rush? There is no such thing as death, so, in truth, we have all the time in the world. It also gets much easier and much more fun the higher you go. The material universe and this schoolhouse called Earth is definitely one of the tougher schools. It will be a big plus on your cosmic resume that you went to planetary college here.

When I say that you have a cosmic resume, this is no joke and not just a metaphor. As you move up this ladder of consciousness, you might be offered jobs in other solar systems, other galaxies, other universes, and other multi-universes. When a given ascended master is gifted at what he does, word gets around. The same is true on a microcosmic level on Earth. This is true in all professions, sports, and/or the spiritual movement. The same is true in the solar system, galaxy, universe, and multi-universe.

Other solar, galactic or universal hierarchies might offer you job opportunities you can't refuse, not because of the money they offer you but because of the service and growth potential. There is no competition between galaxies, for example, because God is the guiding force for all. On that level, what you choose will be God's will. There are, in truth, unlimited opportunities for your particular service skills.

There are vast cycles of evolution involving the in-breath and out-breath of Brahma. For example, I mentioned earlier an occult century is one hundred years of Brahma. In the Alice Bailey books, Djwhal Khul said that this period of time constitutes the whole period of Brahma's age, which is esoterically referred to as a *mahakalpa*.

You think one Cosmic Day is long, being 4.3 billion years and then another 4.3 billion years for a Cosmic Night. A mahakalpa is 311 trillion, 40 billion years. To put this in perspective, humankind has only been on the Earth, according to Edgar Cayce, for 10.5 million years. Sanat Kumara has been the Planetary Logos for 18.5 million years. We are talking about trillions and billions of years!

This book would not be complete without integrating the view of the cosmos from *The Urantia Book*. Because many people might be reading this book before reading some of my others, I am quoting two paragraphs from my book *Hidden Mysteries*.

The Urantia Book, for those of you who are not familiar with it, is another book that is truly a revelation of God. It was written by a commission of universal beings who reside in the capital of our super-universe. In their writings they refer to Earth as "Urantia." The following paragraphs describe the physical organization of the universe as depicted in *The Urantia Book*:

Your world, Urantia, is one of many similar inhabited planets that comprise the local universe of "Nebadon." This universe, together with similar creations, make up the super-universe of "Orvonton," from evolutionary super-universes of time and space that circle the never-beginning, never-ending creation of divine perfection—the central universe of "Havona." At the heart of this eternal and central universe is the stationary "Isle of Paradise," the geographic center of infinity and the dwelling place of the Eternal God.

The seven evolving super-universes, in association with the central and divine universe, we commonly refer to as the "grand universe." These are the now organized and inhabited creations. They are all a part of the master universe, which also embraces the uninhabited but mobilizing universes of outer space [excerpted from *Hidden Mysteries,* this information is sourced from *The Urantia Book*].

As I began to meditate on this description what I realized is that the entire infinite universe is like one gigantic atom. The stationary Isle of Paradise is the only stationary point in all of Creation. Hence, it is like the nucleus of the atom. The super-universes, universes, galaxies and solar systems are like the electrons, protons and neutrons.

Djwhal Khul once told me that the monad had a nucleus to it. This made sense to me, for the microcosm is like the macrocosm. To look at the smallest physical particle in the material universe is to get a glimpse of God at the macrocosmic level also.

The Urantia Book also states that the physical universe extends infinitely. The stationary Isle of Paradise is not a time creation, but an eternal existence. It is the perfect and eternal nucleus of the master universe. The master universe includes all that I have told you about so far and also embraces the uninhabited but mobilizing universes of outer space. *The Urantia Book* then divides the outer space regions into four levels: first, second, third and fourth.

The fifth level is called "open space." It states that the grand universe has an aggregate evolutionary potential of seven trillion inhabited planets. The grand universe includes everything in the universe except for the outer space levels just mentioned. There is potential for even more inhabited planets if the outer space levels are included. Our particular universe of Nebadon is one of the new universes in God's creation. It lies on the outer edge of the grand universe.

So, our universe is on the outer edge, from the geographic or physical standpoint, of the center of the universe. From a spiritual standpoint, this has no bearing on how close or far we are to God because time and space is really only an illusion of linear time.

More on Universal Evolution

One by one, every universe in God's creation will ascend just as every individual will. We can visit these other universes in the dream state. I remember one night I was taken to the Govinda galaxy in the dream state. I was told that I was given this experience to accelerate my ascension and permanently anchor the love vibration. Each universe and galaxy has a different vibration. Ask in meditation or in the dream state to be taken by the Masters to visit another universe to see how it feels. We can visit other universes all we want, but we are not allowed to permanently leave this universe until we graduate.

I am not sure whether or not the cosmology of *The Urantia Book* concerning the organization of the physical universe is true. I will say it is very interesting food for thought. I like the idea of there being a stationary Isle of Paradise. It sounds like Shamballa on a cosmic level. I think this would make another really good *Star Trek* movie.

I then asked Melchizedek why this process of incarnation into matter began. I asked whether this was our choice or if we had to do this as part of God's plan. Melchizedek smiled on the inner plane and then with his quick wit said, "It seemed like a good idea at the time." He said that God's plan was to extend God's kingdom into the dense vibration. In essence, this was an experiment that was greatly determined by the use of our free choice or free will.

I then asked Melchizedek what will happen when all souls return not only to Melchizedek, but on a larger scale, all the way back to God. He said immediately that there is the in-breath and out-breath again. Once God has breathed all souls back into His heart there will emerge a new ultimate evolutionary cycle with a new theme at a much higher level—a new creative experiment begins. The difference being, however, that we have returned home conscious.

Previous to this in our creation we were not conscious in the same way we are now or will be after traversing planetary, solar, galactic, universal and multi-universal levels to return home again. Eventually we will integrate and absorb universes in a way similar to how we now absorb our eleven other soul extensions or 144 monadic soul extensions, which enable us to ascend.

Do you see here how the microcosm is like the macrocosm? Melchizedek is the archetypal being to which we are all heading for our universe. From what we were given in this session, he is in charge of the forty-three other universes from the Source of our Cosmic Day. The exact number forty-three might not be completely accurate, however, this is not important. When one goes to the multi-universal level ascension seat, one is tapping into the essence of these universes, which is why this is so profound.

I had previously thought that Melchizedek was in charge of all forty-three universes (or whatever number it is). Melchizedek is in charge of only our universe but does sit on the Multi-universal Council, since he is one of the Universal Logoi.

Well, Melchizedek is the ultimate, fully integrated universal archetype, who is our ultimate leader and president, so to speak. So, there is a being that we will refer to as the Source of this Cosmic Day, who is in charge of coordinating the many universes that make up the multi-universal level. There are infinite numbers of sources who then report to God, the ultimate Source.

The evolution of a universe is, of course, dependent on the evolution of the astronomical number of galaxies, solar systems, planets and incarnated souls that make up a given planetary system. Each individual soul is like a cell in the universe—each country a molecule; each planet a grouping of cells; each solar system a part of an organ system; each galaxy like an organ or gland; the entire universe, the full body of Melchizedek. The multi-universe has many individual bodies. At the highest cosmic level is the infinite number of bodies that make up the omnipresent, omnipotent and omniscient body of God, who contains and expresses through them all.

When a universe ascends, in a sense it merges with the Multi-universal Source at the next level above itself before the Source of our Cosmic Day breathes out another universe. All the infinite number of universes in God's body are evolving at a different rate of speed.

Again, as I mentioned in *Beyond Ascension,* some universes are closed down early and brought into the cosmic laboratory and completed, because the theme of that particular universe was not working. The example that Vywamus once gave was the reading of a bad book. Why continue reading it? The Source closes it down and completes it in the cosmic laboratory and makes the ensuing knowledge and wisdom gained available to all. Vywamus said that ten universes were closed down from the Source of our Cosmic Day in 1988 [see "The Twenty-Four Dimensions of Reality" in *Beyond Ascension*].

Currently, we are in a cosmic in-breath cycle, which means we are all returning to Source. There obviously is no rush, but there is a big push by the "powers that be" in the cosmos to make as much progress as possible given that we have completed three-quarters of our current Cosmic Day and have only one-quarter left.

From our perspective, the 1.2 billion years left seems like an eternity given that humanity has only lived on Earth for 10.5 million years. From the perspective of the Source of our Cosmic Day, it is like thinking in terms of possibly millions of occult centuries, which again is one hundred years of Brahma to us. One twenty-four hour day seems like a long time to us, but a day for the Source is 8.6 billion years. A lifetime for us is one hundred years. A lifetime for the Source of our Cosmic Day is 311 trillion, 40 billion years.

As you can see, everything is relative. One begins to get a sense of how minuscule he/she really is in the whole scheme of things, yet still very important because God's plan will not be complete unless every cell is working properly.

There is a cosmic time relationship to everything. For example, what happens if one of Melchizedek's organs is not functioning as well as the rest of his organs are? Organs are like galaxies. This is, in a sense, fouling up the timetable for the entire universal ascension. Melchizedek will then send one of his emergency teams from the Order of Melchizedek to rectify this situation. This is kind of what is going on with the Earth and our solar system. There is a big push to move it forward after 3.2 billions years of rather slow progress in the Cosmic Day. The Earth will make more progress in the forty-year time cycle from 1988 to 2028 than it did previously in 3.2 billion years. This is a mind-boggling concept and this accelerated progress is why it is such a blessing to be incarnated in this school at this time.

Each and every universe has to complete its cosmic theme whether through the infinite number of Cosmic Days or by being taken into the cosmic laboratory for completion. God's infinite universe is like a gigantic puzzle, and if a particular universe is not completed, it is like a puzzlepiece is missing from God's divine plan. On a lower level, this would be the same as thinking that the universe could ascend without one of its galaxies. On an even lower scale, the galaxy can't ascend without all its solar systems, nor can a solar system ascend without all its planets ascending. Our planet can't ascend without every soul ascending.

In our planet, there are 60 million monads. This means 60 million times 144 to get the number of soul extensions or personalities in the process of incarnation. This is because each monad, or Mighty I Am Presence, has 144 personalities connected to it in its monadic family, as I have explained in *The Complete Ascension Manual.*

Our solar system has two planets that have now ascended: Venus, which is the most advanced, and Earth, which has most recently advanced. Just as the universe deals with mahakalpas, or occult centuries dealing with one hundred years of Brahma, the Earth deals with smaller cycles that are connected with the seven root races. Each root race is connected with the evolvement of one chakra for humanity, beginning at the base.

We are currently in the fifth root race, which is the Aryan race. It has taken us 18.5 million years to work through just five root races. The Meruvian root race is just now beginning to cycle in. Each root race is also connected to a certain soul quality. The Aryan root race, which we have currently been in, is connected with mental development. In the Atlantean time it was emotional development. Personality development and intuition are now coming in on a mass scale.

The advanced initiates on this planet are much further ahead of the mass consciousness, which (of course) is good. Helios is the Solar Logos and is in charge of the ascension process of the solar system. The Planetary Logos of each of the nine planets in our solar system work for Helios and are like chakras in his body.

Helios works for Melchior, who is the Galactic Logos, and is in charge of helping the galaxy to ascend. The most advanced civilization in our Milky Way galaxy is Arcturus. This is why the Earth is now beginning to work so closely with the Arcturians.

In regard to our solar system, there is a term called "sacred planet status." A planet in our solar system achieves this status when it takes its third initiation, or soul merge. So one can see that planets take initiations the same way humans do. This initiation process also applies to solar systems, galaxies and universes, but, of course, with different standards for achieving their initiations.

Melchizedek, who runs our universe, reports to the Source of our Cosmic Day and sits on one of the councils of the Cosmic Council of Twelve, which runs the infinite universe. Just as our solar system, for example, is a Second Ray solar system and our planet a Fourth Ray planet, our universe on a macrocosmic level is made up of one of the cosmic rays.

The elder that Melchizedek reports to is the member of the Cosmic Council of Twelve in charge of the cosmic ray (not planetary ray) under whose auspices our universe falls. Remember that each one of the twelve members of the Cosmic Council of Twelve, which runs God's infinite universe, is in charge of one cosmic ray.

In this sense, the infinite universe is divided into twelve sections. We see this on a microcosmic and planetary level in the study of astrology, which has the twelve signs of the zodiac, in the twelve major archetypes, in the twelve planetary rays and in the twelve planets; nine exoteric and three hidden. Even though Melchizedek said there are an infinite number of sources for Cosmic Days and universes, they all fall under one of these twelve cosmic rays. Now, there might be a process of exploring one of the other cosmic ray externalizations after we return to Source and achieve our cosmic ascension, but we will each achieve our cosmic ascension on *one* cosmic ray.

There might be an aspect of the ultimate cosmic plan in which one would take twelve different cosmic ascensions, one on each ray. This would give one a complete experience of God on all twelve cosmic rays and levels. I am not completely sure on this, however, we did receive information on such a concept. This would deal with the future in-breaths and out-breaths of God.

The nature of these other cosmic ascensions would be very different from our experience here, for we would be on a different cosmic ray theme. It would also be a more evolved understanding and experience because of already having achieved one cosmic ascension. I received information that the core group and I are working on our third cosmic ascension.

What we are really dealing with here is cosmic astrology, not planetary astrology. One would be taking cosmic ascensions in the twelve cosmic signs, or twelve cosmic rays. Then one has achieved ultimate cosmic ascension and can serve at full God potential, capacity and maturity on all cosmic rays in all cosmic zodiac signs. God's divine plan will not be complete until all souls achieve this. When this is all complete, knowing God, He/She will probably create a new cosmic divine plan. So, what we are dealing with here is a new concept of what I am now terming "ultimate cosmic ascension."

Melchizedek also told us that just as monads group together in their work on this planet, universes also group together. In this sense we have neighboring universes. I have spoken of this in *Beyond Ascension* as the forty-three Christed universes from the Source of our Cosmic Day (Melchizedek tells me that number might not be right, but the concept is sound). Besides the fact that we are connected to all the universes by the Source of our Cosmic Day, we are also connected to all the universes by the Cosmic Council of Twelve member who is in charge of our particular universe and cosmic ray. There might also be a grouping of cosmic rays and cosmic members of the Council of Twelve in a particular quadrant, so to speak, of the cosmos.

I know that on a more microcosmic level this concept applies in terms of our galaxy. Our galaxy, under the guidance of Melchior, is divided into four quadrants. I intuitively believe that this same principle applies on the cosmic levels as well. If it is true that there are, in a sense, twelve cosmic ascensions prior to full ultimate cosmic ascension, then I am sure there is a certain grouping of cosmic ray ascension masters first.

Metaphorically, like a pie divided equally four ways, each quarter of the pie would have three cosmic ascensions in it. So, in a greater sense, we would also be connected to all universes in each cosmic quarter. This gets complicated, however, because we are not just dealing here with the material universe, but also with multi-dimensional realities. But this might be one good model for looking at this.

I spoke of Extraterrestrial visitation; however, there can also be soul and spirit travel visitation by us to other universes and by other universal beings to ours. I wouldn't do this without the help of Melchizedek and without a good spiritual reason for doing it. If going there is not helpful to your spiritual progress then why go? Leave this up to Melchizedek to decide, for this is obviously beyond each of our comprehensions to know at this level of our development.

The three cosmic rays and cosmic ascension paths that are grouped together may share similar cosmic themes as to their expression. This is much like an astrological horoscope, with the three forming a type of trinity.

Just as people on Earth, once achieving and fully realizing their ascension, have the potential to ultimately be able to raise their body by dematerialization into light, the same is true for the planet, solar system, galaxy and all galaxies in Melchizedek's universe. It still has existence, but at a higher dimension of reality as it evolves upward.

This applies to the physical planet as well as the beings living on the planet. Arcturus is an example of this. It was once a planet like ours, but now exists at a much higher level of density because of its evolvement. (I suggest reading Norma Milanovich's book, *We, the Arcturians,* as well as my books *Beyond Ascension* and *Hidden Mysteries,* in which there are chapters on the Arcturians.)

Melchizedek commented humorously on the incredible amount of time of these cosmic cycles when he said, "What else do you have to do?" He then said, "You can rush to get it done and all God is going to do is breathe you back out again." The point was obviously to keep it all in perspective and to enjoy ourselves.

One other interesting point that Melchizedek made about this process is that there is a simultaneity to the initiation process. He said that with all the spiritual work we are doing with him and on the inner plane in meditation and sleep time, we are picking up many different energies simultaneously. We are also anchoring and activating higher chakras, bodies and light quotient.

We are laying the foundation in a profound way to make future initiations much easier, even though we haven't taken those initiations yet. I was happy to hear from Melchizedek that for our process we might triple or quadruple this number to get a true sense of the current intensity.

The guidance that comes to me as I say this is that the first seven initiations are the slowest because they are tied to material existence. The fact that the rest of the initiations will not be tied to matter will speed things up enormously and nonlinear space and time realities will be the norm. So, in a sense, there is the possibility to work on many initiations simultaneously, for the process is not quite as linear as we conceive it now from the Earthsphere perspective and phase that we are currently in.

I again asked Djwhal Khul about the issue of the existence of previous solar systems. This question arose because of his statement in the Alice Bailey book *The Rays and the Initiations* in which he said that the Jewish race was the most advanced root race from the previous solar system. I have never fully understood what this meant. What Djwhal Khul seemed to indicate is that a new solar system begins when the evolutionary process of the seven root races has been completed. In the back of my mind I can't help but think that there might be more to this statement than this.

This whole subject of the globes, the rounds, and the schemes is an area of understanding that I have not yet been able to decipher. Sometimes I need to understand a subject more clearly before the Masters can bring through more obscure information. The old Theosophical books that were supposed to have information on it were not all available anymore.

The conclusion that I have arrived at is that one day of Brahma equals one round. One week of Brahma equals seven rounds, which make up one scheme. One year of Brahma equals seven planetary schemes, which is somehow connected to the seven chains. One hundred years of Brahma equals an occult century, which is the period of a solar system.

In going through this I think I might have answered my own question. Each solar system is one hundred years of Brahma. Therefore, what I first said about the seven root races is not true, as my intuition was telling me. I think the seven root races would be more like one hour of Brahma. Even though one hour of Brahma might not seem like a long time, in truth, this could translate to 30 or 40 million years of our time. What we have here are cycles within cycles, within cycles, within cycles. My mechanical mind would love to figure out how this all works. Yet in this moment I am getting this with my intuitive mind; however, my left brain is not yet completely satisfied.

I will continue to research this concept. What I now realize is that the information I received from Djwhal Khul refers to the completion of a planetary cycle. This is what he thought I was asking, but the completion of a whole solar system is a much, much, much longer cycle made up of millions of planetary cycles, or the completion of seven root race cycles.

So, to go through seven solar systems, which is another longer cycle, would take 700 years of Brahma. Again, remember, just one day of Brahma is 4.3 billion years. It would take seven occult centuries to complete a solar system cycle, which again is a smaller cycle within a larger cycle of the evolution of a galaxy. As we evolve and become masters on solar, galactic and universal levels, this is the cosmic science we will study. As planetary masters we are currently focused mainly on the planetary cycles. Once we fully master this we will be ready to contemplate the solar system, the solar science and on upward, until eventually understanding the cosmic science of the entire infinite universe.

The Seven Root Races				
Root Race	Continent	Attunement	Chakra	Yoga
1. Polarian	The Imperishable Sacred Land	Physical	1st chakra	Hatha yoga
2. Hyperborean	Continent of Hyperborea	Physical	1st chakra	Hatha yoga
3. Lemurian	Continent of Lemuria	Physical	2nd chakra	Hatha yoga
4. Atlantean	Continent of Atlantis	Emotional	3rd chakra	Bhakti yoga
5. Aryan	Europe, Asia Minor, America	Mental	4th chakra	Raja yoga
6. Meruvian	North America	Personality	5th chakra	Agni yoga
7. Paradisian	Tara	Soul	6th chakra	Unknown

The Sacred Planets

I mentioned earlier the fact that a planet is termed "sacred" once it has attained the third, or soul merge, initiation. The following is an updated look at our solar system in terms of which planets have attained at least this initiation level. This gives us a sense of the evolvement level of our solar system. The following chart is from Alice Bailey's *The Rays and the Initiations*.

The Sacred Planets and Their Rays

Earth	Ray IV
Vulcan	Ray I
Mercury	Ray IV
Venus	Ray V
Jupiter	Ray II
Saturn	Ray III
Neptune	Ray VI
Uranus	Ray VII

The Non-sacred Planets and Their Rays

Mars	Ray VI
Pluto	Ray I
The Moon	Ray IV
(veiling a hidden planet)	
The Sun	Ray II
(veiling a hidden planet)	

I mentioned earlier that Earth and Venus were the only planets to have taken their ascension in our solar system. Djwhal Khul told me that

Jupiter was the next planet that was getting close to taking its ascension, which I found very interesting, as Jupiter has to do with expansiveness and transcending the negative ego.

A Footnote from Melchizedek

After completing this chapter, I was running a few last things by Melchizedek when he asked me to put one footnote or qualification on the information I have presented regarding the twelve cosmic ascensions leading to ultimate cosmic ascension. What he told me is that this was most definitely the model he wanted me to present as representative of his teachings; however, he wanted me to add to this model that "God is not limited."

He gave the example of the twelve major archetypes, which each have hundreds of sub-archetypes. For categorization purposes and clarification, we have divided them into the twelve sub-archetypes. Melchizedek said that in a similar way the twelve cosmic ascensions could have such subdivisions, given that there are twelve cosmic rays and twelve elders who sit on the Cosmic Council of Twelve. The number twelve is the most accurate model for mapping the cosmos. He said, however, that God is infinite and cannot be limited by any model. Melchizedek definitely wanted me to present this model, but who knows, there might be 144 cosmic ascensions through other universal ascensions or six million or infinite numbers of them.

I say "infinite" in the sense that even though there is definitely a cosmic ascension that is achieved, just as there is a planetary ascension, there is no ceiling on evolution. Maybe the twelve cosmic ascensions are the ultimate completion of the ascension process, but growth still continues after this point. There are always higher and higher levels of refinement and purity that can be focused upon. We must be open to the fact that there could be more then twelve cosmic in-breaths and out-breaths of God. There is some kind of completion point between the fifth and seventh cosmic plane. There will be a place of basic total completion; however, refined growth and service will continue.

I also asked Melchizedek about how our galaxy was evolving in terms of all the galaxies in our Melchizedek universe. The only thing I could get out of the Grand Master was that our Milky Way galaxy was neither the most advanced nor the least advanced in his universe, but somewhere in the middle. I was glad to hear that at least we aren't a backward galaxy holding up the progression of the universal ascension. (As one shifts to a cosmic citizen focus, thoughts such as this enter one's mind.)

Melchizedek and Djwhal Khul also said that in regard to ultimate cosmic ascension, which is indeed a reality, there might be a way of absorbing these other cosmic in-breaths and out-breaths connected with the cosmic rays in a way that is different from going back into physical existence. There is a possibility that they might just be integrated from the Source level. Once cosmic ascension is achieved, absorption of other cosmic ascension paths most probably may not be done in the incarnational process we have just experienced.

Djwhal Khul said that this school or universe we are in is the "hardball" school. That is why the theme of this Cosmic Day is "Courage." It is one of the hardest schools of all. The most important thing to understand here is that there is a point of attainment of comic ascension; however, growth, expansion, creativity, and service is infinite.

6

The Twenty-Four
Dimensions of Reality

One of the most confusing subjects for any seeker on the spiritual path is the subject of the dimensions of reality and planes of consciousness. Djwhal Khul, in his writings through Alice Bailey, has spoken of the seven subplanes of the cosmic physical through which all are evolving—the physical, astral, mental, Buddhic, atmic, monadic, and logoic. Once you evolve through these seven subplanes of the cosmic physical plane you must then evolve through the seven cosmic planes, which have the exact same names as the seven subplanes, but they are cosmic in nature instead of just subplanes of the first cosmic physical plane. Each of the seven major initiations through which all must evolve on this plane are associated with the seven subplanes of the cosmic physical plane:

First initiation	Mastery of the physical plane
Second initiation	Mastery of the astral plane
Third initiation	Mastery of the mental plane
Fourth initiation	Anchoring of the Buddhic plane
Fifth initiation	Anchoring of the atmic plane

Sixth initiation	Full anchoring of the monadic plane
Seventh initiation	Full anchoring of the logoic plane

What gets very confusing is that there are not only these seven planes of consciousness and seven cosmic planes of consciousness that make up the three hundred fifty-two levels of the Mahatma; they also make up the three hundred fifty-two levels of initiation needed to return completely to the Godhead at the highest level. There are also ten dimensions of reality that all human beings are working with which are different from these seven planes. I am sure this chapter will be of great value for I know how confused I have been when terms such as fourth, fifth, and sixth dimensions have been thrown around. For example, at ascension, you merge with the monadic plane, which is also merged with the fifth dimension. The dimensions do not coincide with the seven subplanes.

It was really Vywamus who finally helped me to understand the dimensions. This understanding began to come forth in the process of many long conversations I had with him. Vywamus also guided me to read his book *Scopes of Dimensions,* channeled by Janet McClure, which was invaluable. The only problem was that after reading it I still didn't understand the dimensions completely so I had to go back to Vywamus to have him explain them further and answer all my questions, which he was kind enough and patient enough to do. Vywamus, the higher self of Sanat Kumara, has brought forth some of the most profound information ever given to humanity on this subject. I am going to attempt here to explain it in the most simple terms possible. My profound "thank you" to Vywamus for all his help on this subject and to Janet McClure for her groundbreaking work in this area.

The First Dimension

The key term for the first dimension is "completion." It is a passageway or a corridor that leads to some kind of completion. Any time you complete a project in your life you are accessing the first dimension. This feeling of completion stimulates a flow of energy that leads to the second dimension.

The Second Dimension

The key word for the second dimension is "new beginnings." Once you complete something it leads to an automatic desire to begin something new, sometimes even before fully completing the previous project. An example of this might be the initiation process. You might be in the process of completing your fifth initiation, but you are already thinking about beginning your sixth initiation and ascension. The example could also be more mundane, such as finishing up high school but already beginning to take a few college courses.

It is the first dimension and a person's response to it that stimulates a connection to the second dimension. I am sure you can relate to this process. As soon as I complete a project or a certain phase of my life I automatically begin thinking about what I am going to focus on next. This process is accessing the first two dimensions of reality.

The Third Dimension

You are more familiar with the third dimension. The key term here, according to Vywamus, is "magnification." Magnification is like densification. The third dimension vibrates at literally one-tenth the frequency of Source, or God. That is why, after completing the seven levels of initiation and fully ascending, you are still only one-tenth of the way up a ten-inch ruler in terms of the total scope of your spiritual path back to the Godhead. The slow rate of vibration explains why everything looks solid in the third dimension when, in truth, nothing is solid but merely looks so to your physical eyes, which perceive a very narrow frequency band. The reason God and the creator gods (Elohim) have slowed the material universe ten-fold is so that it can be taken apart, studied, and then put back together. The third dimension is a slowed creative flow that allows you to see all of Creation through a type of mirroring process. It is, in a sense, a practice area for apprentice gods.

Once humanity has shown itself responsible in this slow dimension, it will then be allowed to create in the more rarefied dimensions of reality. The interesting thing is that planet Earth, as of the Harmonic Convergence in 1987, has moved into the fourth dimension. Vywamus and Djwhal Khul have said that each dimension has a scale from one to one hundred. Planet Earth is now at level one or two—the very beginning stages of the fourth dimension. That is why planet Earth is now considered a sacred planet, esoterically speaking.

The Fourth Dimension

The key term for the fourth dimension is "flow." Everything flows more smoothly and evenly and in a deeper fashion than in the third dimension. The third dimension has a type of flow, but it does not have depth and gets stuck and jammed up very easily. The fourth-dimensional flow has a stability that allows it to flow easily even during the storms of life. This flow operates on physical, emotional, mental, and spiritual levels.

An example of the increased flow, Vywamus said, is that professional athletes will begin to break all records that existed when Earth functioned as a planet in the third dimension because of the way the fourth dimension allows a greater flow, even at the physical level. This flow will operate on the emotional, mental, and spiritual levels in the same way. There will be greater flow among people on the planet as a whole, which was evidenced by the downfall of Communism and the end of apartheid in South Africa.

It is also occurring in our personal lives. The fourth dimension is more continuous and more like a circle. The emotional body is the resident guide for the fourth dimension. The resident guide for the third dimension is the physical body, for the fifth dimension, the mental body, for the sixth dimension, the spiritual body. Although this is true, it is essential for all the bodies to be able to access all the dimensions, despite having a dimension or dimensions to which they relate to the best.

Humanity is now beginning to learn to create its base, its foundation, in the fourth dimension instead of in the third dimension. Obviously, this process is not complete yet, but it is beginning to happen.

The Fifth Dimension

The key term for the fifth dimension is "divine structure" or "ideal structure." It is the structural blueprinting system. The fifth dimension is the dimension with which you merge at your sixth initiation and ascension. An example of this structural blueprinting system is that at ascension, the mayavarupa body, or monadic blueprint body, is fully anchored into your physical vehicle. In other words, you are then operating entirely out of the monadic blueprint and not out of a blueprint tainted by all your past incarnations. At ascension you are totally merged with your ideal structure forevermore.

The resident expert, again, is the mental body. The fifth dimension deals with divine order and with the building blocks with which creation takes place. The sixth dimension brings forth the concept, but it is the fifth dimension that executes the plans.

The Sixth Dimension

The key term for the sixth dimension is "complete understanding." You merge with the sixth dimension when you take your seventh initiation, which is the full completion of the seven levels of initiation that can be taken on this Earthly plane. The sixth initiation brings the first major contact with the Galactic Core, which is fully realized in the seventh dimension. The sixth dimension is also the circuitry system that ensures there is divine current to meet all of the dimensional structures' needs. The sixth dimension also has a connection with the ninth dimension from where, Vywamus told me, this whole process is programmed. The Galactic Core inputs into the sixth dimension in a way that allows beings on Earth to begin a more complete usage of the dimensions. There is also a restimulation of energy on the sixth dimension from the ninth, eighth, and seventh dimensions of reality so that that energy can flow directly into dimensions one through five. The electrical flow of the energy the fifth dimension uses in its blueprinting system is generated from the sixth dimension.

The Seventh Dimension

The key term for the seventh dimension is "expansion." The seventh dimension is a turnaround point for inner and outer experiences. It is a corridor that allows you to reframe the way you experience the dimensional structures. It allows for experiential objectivity. The seventh dimension is a dimensional reality you can go to to take a look at how well you have manifested the ideal. The experiential objectivity you gain from this perspective will stimulate new ideas upon which you can then expand in other-dimensional realities.

The Eighth Dimension

The key term for the eighth dimension is "potentiality." The eighth dimension is the area that contains all potentialities. Potentialities are tried out and experimented with in the eighth dimension. This brings up the fascinating subject of "cosmic days." A cosmic day is a conceptual framework within which the Source may completely explore a particular theme.

The theme of planet Earth's cosmic day is "courage." A cosmic day lasts for 4.3 billion years; 3.1 billion years of this cosmic day have already passed, so there are still 1.2 billion years left. Humanity has been on Earth for only about 18.5 million years. When a cosmic day is completed, the particular Source who is in charge of that cosmic day pulls it back in. This has been referred to as a "cosmic night." It could last for another 4.3 billion years or not, depending on the Source.

Humanity's Source is currently in charge of fifty-one different cosmic days. What sometimes happens is that a cosmic day based on a particular theme in a particular universe does not work out as planned. It is like a book you are reading but after having read a quarter of it you find it is boring and not going anywhere. Then the Source ends the cosmic day prematurely and sends it back to the "laboratory" in the eighth dimension in a sort of miniaturized form. That particular cosmic day is reworked and then brought to completion.

The eighth dimension is a kind of cosmic laboratory in which ideas coming from the ninth dimension are first tried out to see if they will work. When cosmic days are brought to completion and proper resolution in miniaturized form, it is possible for humans and for the Earth as a whole to access this Divine knowledge.

It must be stated here that most of the accessing of the seventh, eighth, and ninth dimensions of reality occurs during sleep time. It is possible to request, before bed, the retention of this information for your own personal evolution and also for service to others.

In Janet McClure's book *Scopes of Dimensions,* Vywamus tells of a most extraordinary recent occurrence in regard to the Source that Earth's Source is merging with. If I am not mistaken, these two Sources are referred to as Melchizedek and Kalmelchizedek. During a sixteen-day period from July 25 to August 10, 1988, no fewer than ten cosmic days were pulled back prematurely because they were not working. All ten were put into a miniaturized state in the eighth-dimensional laboratory and brought to proper resolution. This, to me, seems absolutely extraordinary. This all occurred fairly close to the Harmonic Convergence and this planet's movement into the fourth dimension. It is beginning to become clear now what an amazing time that really was. The themes and withdrawal dates of those ten cosmic days were:

1. Unlimited Energy	July 25, 1988
2. Parallels of Love	July 26, 1988
3. Joyous Beginnings	July 26, 1988
4. Balancing of Oppositions	July 28, 1988
5. Integration	July 30, 1988
6. Unlimited Communication	July 31, 1988
7. Surrender to the Plan	August 3, 1988
8. Sacrifice	August 6, 1988
9. Unconditional Love	August 7, 1988
10.Joyous Movement	August 10, 1988

I find it absolutely fascinating to note the themes of other cosmic days. My understanding is that this cosmic day of courage is not in danger of being called back to Source prematurely. Even if it were, there is nothing to fear, for a cosmic night is like an incubation period before a new expansion. It is expanding and contracting or is, in truth, the "in-breath and outhreath of Brahma."

The key point here is that you are able to use the strengths that are developed in the cosmic laboratories in the eighth dimension even when a cosmic day is prematurely closed down. It makes a lot of sense when you think about it. Why continue a cosmic day if it is not really working out? God, in a sense, is stopping unnecessary suffering and unfulfillment. Life is eternal, as there is always another cosmic day. There are infinite numbers of cosmic days and Sources who are in charge of them.

The ending of the ten cosmic days affected not only the Earth but also the entire cosmos. The eighth-dimensional laboratory also tries out cosmic day ideas from the ninth dimension to see if they will allow the theme ascribed to them to flow creatively and expand. One of the key lessons here is to see that even God learns from His mistakes and is constantly creating, expanding, and adjusting His creations in a most unlimited fashion. Vywamus has provided a glimpse of the true nature of reality at the cosmic levels. I think you will agree it is quite mind-boggling, especially given the fact that there is no time and space at these levels so everything is happening multi-dimensionally and simultaneously.

The goal of creation is to expand whatever theme is being explored. If it is not working, close it down, fix it in miniaturized form in the eighth dimension, and try something new. It feels to me like God is having a lot of fun. You get a sense here of the unlimitedness and the creativity of the Godforce. Vywamus has said that the full purpose of creation is simply joyous expression, a loving exercise in creativity.

The eighth dimension is the most expansive of the dimensions, as you can see from all the potentialities that are experimented with there. I am personally very taken with how God is so creative on these cosmic levels and obviously not fearful in the slightest of making mistakes. The traditional view of God in most religions is that God, being perfect, is incapable of anything but perfection. I have a feeling that God does not even look at closing down cosmic days prematurely as being mistakes. It feels more like unlimited creativity and having fun. Life is eternal, so what does it matter?

When cosmic days are ended and brought back to the eighth-dimensional laboratory, they are often played out in miniaturized form to see where they would have gone if allowed to continue. God learns more about Himself and then appropriate adjustments can be made for future cosmic days. The resolution of cosmic days in this miniaturized form is a cosmic substitute for the actual physical experience, which humans can tap into and use. Vywamus said that the Source will always finish and compile all cosmic days and bring them to proper resolution. It is just a question of whether it is done in actual experience or is completed in the eighth-dimensional laboratory. So you could say it is not really a mistake, it is just a transfer of dimensions for the completion of God's Divine Plan.

The Ninth Dimension

The key word for the ninth dimension is "co-creation." The ninth dimension is the administration level for all the dimensions. It is also the think-tank for the co-creator level where the conception of existence takes place; that is, the experiential side of existence. True divine beingness lies far beyond any dimensional structure. Vywamus told me that at the very highest level there is the Creator level; then comes the co-creator level where there are twelve co-creator gods. You usually end up working for one of these co-creator gods, although you are not limited, by any means.

The ninth dimension is the Source's overall viewing level and the home territory of the co-creator levels. Each of you has a part that lives at each of these levels and at all three hundred fifty-two levels of the Mahatma, all the way back to Source. The ninth dimension is the entrance to your full cosmic evolution. It is the last stage before leaving the cosmic physical universe, you might say. It is the entrance to the full scope of the three hundred fifty-two levels of the Mahatma. The understanding that a part of you already exists on all the higher levels, even back up to the Creator level, means that, in one sense, you have already achieved full completion and reunion with the Godhead. You are, in truth, already there. The problem is that you haven't fully realized it yet—that is the process of initiation and evolution.

Vywamus has told me that at higher levels of evolution you will not look at the initiation process in the same linear way you are seeing it now. Since there is no time and space and you are multi-dimensional, you will be working on all initiations simultaneously.

The ninth dimension is the basic point of Creator contact. The idea is for you to learn to merge with the higher aspects of yourself in the same way that you have learned to merge with your soul and then your monad at ascension. It is a process of merging with higher and higher levels of your true Godself. The Mahatma is the group consciousness being that is the amalgamation of all aspects of self all the way back to the Godhead. The Mahatma would literally be your self, not yet fully realized.

The image that Vywamus gave through Janet McClure for tuning into this energy (in her book *Scopes of Dimensions)* was to imagine sitting on top of a mountain at the perfect temperature and allowing yourself to receive, with the intent of tuning into the ninth dimension. In truth, most of these dimensions are only truly available during sleep, but a subtle or stepped-down experience might be available to meditate upon.

I asked Vywamus if there is any limit or "ring pass not" beyond which you could not soul travel. He told me that at this level the limit is the tenth dimension. It is a built-in system of protection because you are not at a level to comprehend the cosmic planes. That does not mean that you are not totally connected to the Godhead and the cosmic planes, for you are; however, you will probably not soul travel there very much until you expand your level of evolution and initiatory status.

The Earth experience is about dealing primarily with the first six dimensions of reality. After ascension, seven, eight, and nine become more readily available. My intuition tells me that there might be exceptions to this; I am thinking of certain revelations of God people on the Earth plane have had that go beyond, I believe, soul and monad. Vywamus said that does ring true, however, because it can clearly be seen that progress in service and in the initiation process occurs gradually. You first work yourself, then on the soul level, then on the monadic level serving the planet, then the solar system, then the galaxy, and then the universe.

Why would you be traveling to the highest cosmic planes when you haven't even mastered the first seven planes? I think you travel to the level you can integrate and use; otherwise, what would be the purpose? There are some that, in meditation, can tap directly into the ninth dimension. Others receive it more subtly. Still others can tap in during sleep. The ninth dimension interacts with all the other dimensions.

I asked Vywamus if it was possible to manifest a ninth-dimensional focus on Earth. He said it was possible, but that it has not happened very often in the history of the Earth. He said it was a good goal to aim for, but it must be remembered that the seventh initiation is the highest initiation that can be taken on this plane, and that is merger with the sixth dimension. Even seventh degree initiates, hence sixth-dimensional beings, are somewhat rare, especially given the fact that in the past most people have physically died after ascending. You would have to merge with your eighth- and ninth-dimensional selves while remaining a seventh degree initiate to do this. Vywamus said that a being at that level would be a luminescent Light, constantly changing. It would be invisible. (I was unclear whether he meant all the time or just some of the time.) The metaphor he used was that of ice, water, and steam—a ninth-dimensional being would be beyond steam.

The Tenth Dimension

The tenth dimension, Vywamus told me, marks the movement beyond physicality. The ninth initiation is the last initiation that can be taken in the cosmic physical universe. After that, the Master leaves the cosmic physical universe altogether and begins the progression through the next six cosmic planes—the cosmic astral, cosmic mental, cosmic Buddhic, cosmic atmic, cosmic monadic, and cosmic logoic planes.

Dimensions Nine through Twelve

Dimensions nine through twelve, especially, and actually dimensions seven through twelve, deal with the galactic level of consciousness. Dimensions nine through twelve also deal with the higher university on Sirius. When you request to go to Lenduce's ashram and visit the ascension seats you are accessing this level, as you are when you travel to Sirius while you sleep to attend classes and when you go to the ascension seat in the Galactic Core.

Dimensions Twelve through Twenty-four

Dimensions twelve through twenty-four deal with the universal levels of consciousness. This is the domain of Melchizedek, the Universal Logos. When you request to be taken to the Golden Chamber of Melchizedek, you are beginning to access these levels. Vywamus told me that Sai Baba is a universal avatar who is accessing dimensions twelve through twenty-four.

The Kabbalah and the Ten Dimensions

The Kabbalah and the Tree of Life are wonderful multi-dimensional tools. The ten sephiroth could be associated with the ten dimensions. The three pillars of the Tree of Life represent the third dimension of reality, the dimension in which humans are anchored and which they call home.

Music, Art, and Other Dimensions

Vywamus has brought forth some fascinating information on music and the dimensions. The music you listen to often carries you into the third, fourth, fifth, and sixth dimensions of reality. "The Star-Spangled Banner" is quite unusual in this regard, for it allows you to access the sixth dimension. Its focus is the fourth dimension, but it is able to integrate all the levels. This dimensional shifting is affected not only by the sound, but also by the words and by the person or persons playing the piece of music.

The greatest musicians are those who can travel interdimensionally. The Angelic Kingdom harvests a great deal of the energy that is created by people listening to concerts. Djwhal Khul has told me the same thing about sports events and other gatherings of all kinds. The energy is gathered and used for the purposes of Sanat Kumara and the Spiritual Hierarchy.

Vywamus told me that Beethoven takes people to the fourth, fifth, and sixth dimensions. Rock concerts usually remain in the third, unless the group is focused on brotherhood in its music, as an occasional group is.

Mozart has an occasional piece of music that takes people to the experience of the seventh dimension, along with the fourth, fifth, and sixth. No piece of music is one-dimensional.

I asked similar questions of Vywamus about the arts. He told me that the Sistine Chapel takes people to the fifth and sixth dimensions. He said certain modern paintings occasionally take people into the seventh dimension. Which dimension you move into is dependent upon two factors: the creator and the experiencer. The more highly evolved you are, the more likely you are to be able to allow yourself to experience the higher dimensions through the catalyzation of a work of art or music.

Watching television, Vywamus said, is usually a third-, fourth- or fifth-dimensional experience; being in nature is a fourth-, fifth-, or sixth-dimensional experience, as is attending lectures.

Sports and Other Dimensions

I was surprised to hear that even sports events can take people into different dimensions. Vywamus said that football unites the third, fourth, and fifth dimensions. Achieving a goal brings forth a feeling of freedom, self-confidence, and accomplishment for both players and fans. The losers create a reality of not achieving a goal and they feel the opposite way.

Dimensions and Vortexes

Another very interesting discussion I had with Vywamus was about vortexes. There are certain vortexes on the planet that could be likened to major and minor chakras. Some of these vortexes have higher-dimensional relationships, such as those in Sedona (Arizona), Egypt, Tibet, Siberia, India, Kenya, and South America (particularly Machu Picchu and Brazil), to name a few. Many of them are seventh-dimensional in nature. One of the most famous is the Bermuda Triangle, which Vywamus said was actually an aberration, or imbalance, caused by the great crystal from Atlantis.

Vywamus said this vortex has a seventh- and eighth-dimensional relationship. He likened it to the wormhole described in *Star Trek*. People, planes, and ships are actually dematerialized and transported through a type of wormhole to another place. I asked Vywamus where, and he said, "Sometimes outside of the solar system." I asked him if they were all alive in a physical sense. He said sometimes they are, and other times they lose their physical bodies.

Vywamus told me there is an eighth-dimensional vortex at the polar ice caps near the entrance to the Hollow Earth. This particular vortex takes you out of the galaxy and is used a great deal by Extraterrestrials. It is natural and is not caused by an aberration, as is the Bermuda Triangle.

The vortexes in Sedona, he told me, are mostly of the fourth, fifth, and sixth dimensions, although one of them is a seventh-dimensional vortex. Most of them are protected by Native Americans. Just as there are major and minor chakras in the human body, so there are the same in the Earth.

More Information on the Ten Dimensions of Reality

The ability to teleport occurs in the fifth and sixth dimensions, with knowledge about it coming from the ninth dimension. It is essential to be able to access all of the dimensions with your physical, emotional, mental, and spiritual bodies. Not to access all dimensions would be like moving into a ten-bedroom house and never entering seven of the rooms. Each dimension gives you the opportunity to access certain strengths. Life mirrors certain inconsistencies to you when dimensions are left out. The key word here is "integration." Each of the four bodies speaks, in a sense, a different language, and each relates to the dimensions differently. Each body has an affinity and a lack of affinity for certain dimensions, and that is fine as long as there is an open flow of communication. Your consciousness needs the information from all four bodies to fully understand and use all ten dimensions.

Earth is now moving into the fourth dimension, which will allow everything on the planet to flow more smoothly and easily. Communication will be more consistent and reach deeper levels of understanding. Transportation will be less problematic; people will learn to teleport. (Teleportation is an example of the physical body's learning to contact the fourth dimension and not stay stuck in the third dimension.) All forms of athletics will be more graceful. There will be a greater link between Earth and the Galactic Core, especially with Melchior who is the Galactic Logos.

Vywamus has said that there is another Earth in the fourth dimension, one in the fifth dimension, and so on, all the way up through all the dimensions. This makes sense because you have a self that already exists and functions in those higher dimensions, so why shouldn't the entire Earth have the same? The idea is to merge the fourth-dimensional, fully realized Earth with the Earth that has just entered the fourth dimension. This process, as you can see, has already begun to happen.

Within the ideal grid system, Vywamus says, the emotional body's homebase will be the fourth dimension and the mental body's homebase will be the fifth dimension. That doesn't mean they won't visit, merge with, and access the other dimensions, just that these are their ideal homebases and their areas of greatest expertise.

The fourth-dimensional Earth will be free of all pollution, for pollution comes from a third-dimensional, stuck perspective. The heating up of the Earth's atmosphere, the greenhouse effect, is another example of that perspective; so is the cellulite so many people carry around in their bodies. Merger with the fourth dimension on planetary and personal levels will allow the energy to flow more freely and clear away the debris caused by holding onto the third-dimensional perspective. Life is mirroring the resistance and signaling the need to move into the fourth dimension with the four-body system.

Each of the four bodies will always be affected by the other bodies' perspectives. It is as though each of the bodies takes parts of the other bodies with it when it attunes to another dimension. The ideal is to create clarity of communication within the four-body system.

If there were no dimensions or dimensional structure, there would never be a way to contact one another or to differentiate parts in any way. The dimensions that God has created are the tools by which you are allowed to use your five senses and four bodies to make contact with others and with the different aspects of life. In Janet McClure's *Scopes of Dimensions,* Vywamus says that, "Source talks to Itself through the dimensions." Without the dimensions, life would be just a kaleidoscope of light and sound with no contact whatsoever. True reality is beyond the dimensions, but the dimensions are used as a way of outpicturing God's Divine Plan.

Vywamus also says that the clearest way to attract a relationship partner is by going to the spiritual level on which the divine blueprint lives. It is there you can make the first contact. That will create a magnetic attraction that can build and extend onto other levels.

I have always said that the best way to meet your spiritual mate is to focus completely on your spiritual path and on service to humanity. When you are totally right with self, right with God, and fulfilled in your spiritual path, that special person will just show up at your doorstep without you even trying. A great many people bond on the sexual level first and then often find they don't blend on all four body levels or on higher-dimensional levels, so connecting on a higher level first is preferable.

I also had a discussion with Vywamus about the parallel Earth realities in other dimensions. It might be said that there are nine different Earths—one in each of the nine dimensions of reality. They are like nine rooms in a house with walls that separate them; you can't see from one to the other. The ideal, ultimately, is for the nine Earths from the nine dimensions of reality to become one Earth. The same could be said for the nine aspects of the self.

When people on Earth occasionally have an experience of revelation, they are usually accessing the galactic or universal plane. They are still only about two inches up the ten-inch ruler of the Source's creation, but for the

Earth, it is a very profound contact. Sai Baba is a walking revelation, for he is a universal avatar.

I asked Vywamus if it is possible to travel all the way back to the Source of all Sources on the highest cosmic plane. He said it is possible if there is an important purpose for doing so, although you might not remember it. It would, however, have an effect on your energy matrix. For the most part, you travel to no higher a level than you can comfortably integrate. You are not going to have a revelation of the Godhead at the highest cosmic plane because you are not at a level where you can integrate or even resonate with that experience. The galactic or universal level would be a big enough stretch. I also asked about the next aspect of self beyond the soul and monad in the communication link with Source. He said it is the "Creator level."

I also asked Vywamus about the status of the cosmic day in which Earth is now involved. I wanted to know if there is any possibility that this cosmic day will be closed down and returned to the eighth dimension for completion. Vywamus said that this cosmic day of courage is working magnificently and there is no reason for it to be ended. He also told me that when a cosmic day is closed down and miniaturized, it does not necessarily affect the physical universe, although sometimes it does. Sometimes the closing down and miniaturizing occurs only on an energetic level. Other times there is a complete deactivation of even the physical level. That would lead to a full cosmic night, or what Vywamus referred to as a "cosmic pause." A cosmic night might or might not last as long as a cosmic day. During a cosmic night, you still exist, but you live in more of a "being" state, a state of reflection and passiveness. Evolvement does not occur in the same way.

I asked Vywamus if the cosmic day and cosmic night applied only to the nine dimensions of reality or to God's entire infinite universe. He said it was applied to all of Creation. He ended the discussion by saying that the macrocosm could be understood by focusing on the microcosm of my physical body and four-body system. As I can focus on certain organs, glands, cells, molecules, atoms, and electrons in my body, so God and the infinite numbers of Sources and cosmic days that make up all of Creation can do the same thing on a much grander scale. As you learn to master yourself, you are being prepared to work on the much larger scale of a planet, star system, galaxy, or universe, which are nothing more than organs, molecules, atoms and electrons in God's body.

People on Earth often feel an energy drain because they are spending too much time concentrating on one dimension to the exclusion of the other dimensions. In this society, it is usually the mental dimension that is overemphasized, although sometimes people also lose energy by focusing too much on the emotional body.

Another way of understanding the dimensions as they relate to the Earth is to look at the ley lines, or grid system, of the Earth. Most of you, I am sure, are familiar with this concept. What most people don't understand is that there are grid lines on all nine levels of Earth, in each of the nine dimensions of reality.

Vywamus says the soul level is required in order to reach the sixth dimension. If you are not attuned to your soul or higher self, you will not be able to access the sixth dimension. A person who has died or ascended and who is living in the seventh dimension will utilize the sixth dimension as the connecting link or relay station to channel to humans on Earth. The angels, in particular, use this system. The angels can actually speak from the fourth dimension, even though they come from dimensions six, seven, and nine.

Conclusion

Once more, I want to acknowledge Janet McClure's wonderful book, *Scopes of Dimensions,* which provided me with a framework upon which to build my discussions with Vywamus. I highly recommend reading this book. It is published by Light Technology Publishing in Sedona.

7

How to Master, Understand and Overcome The 27 Earthly Veils and Restrictions of God

My Beloved Readers, this is a most interesting chapter that explains the 27 basic Earthly veils that GOD has placed upon the people of the Earth and the Earth itself! I have never read in any book, presented in a comprehensive manner, about the veils that GOD has placed on Earth! Most of the time we think of GOD as the being that *removes* all veils! So, the key question is, "Why would GOD and the Cosmic Masters purposely create veils upon the Earth?" This is a most interesting question, which I will now explain before sharing what these 27 Earthly veils of GOD are!

The reason that these 27 Earthly veils and limitations were placed upon the Earth and the people of the Earth began over 18.5 million years ago in Earth's history at the time of Lemuria, which predated Atlantis! This was the first Golden Age of this planet, and is referred to in the Bible as the Edenic state! This was the time on Earth when the Earth and the people of the Earth were more etheric in nature! The world was not as physically dense as it is now. This was also the time that predated mankind's eating of the fruit from the Tree of Good and Evil, which I have also described as thinking with one's negative ego/fear-based/separative mind instead of the Spiritual/Christ/Buddha mind! Prior to this occurrence, the Earth and Earth life was a Garden of Eden! Life was beautiful and all lived in unconditional love, harmony, and there was no separation between Spiritual worlds and the world on Earth! There was no stepping into the world of negative ego duality, only making choices within the Mind of God! This was truly the first Golden Age upon the Earth!

Then came the eating of the fruit from the Tree of Good and Evil, and the choice to think with one's negative ego mind! This was the choice to over-identify with the physical body and to go into illusion, glamour, and maya! People began thinking they were physical bodies instead of God living in a physical body! As this negative ego thinking and feeling spread, the world began to densify and physical bodies began to densify. This was not part of the original plan! Pretty soon most of the world, and all the Sons and Daughters of GOD on it, had fallen asleep! It was 18.5 million years ago that Sanat Kumara and his fellow Kumaras came from Venus to rectify and heal this problem! The Light had almost gone out in this world because the dream of illusion and separation was so strong! The Earthly world and physical bodies became totally physically dense because of mankind's consciousness, and separation seemed more real than ever! A whole new plan had to be created by GOD and the Godforce given this new occurrence and sequence of events that had taken place!

Twenty-seven new plans, veils, and limitations were set up over a period of time to deal with this situation! The reason for the 27 plans, veils, and limitations that were instituted was that mankind's consciousness was of such a low vibration, and so run by negative ego thinking, that the planet and all its people had to be put in a kind of "Spiritual Playpen"! Much as a child who is acting out needs lots of structure, limitations and rules until they are proven worthy to be more responsible, the Sons and Daughters of God could not be trusted with their full God powers and abilities, for if they had them they would be used by the negative ego mind and massive destruction would have taken place to the person, the Earth, and even our solar system, galaxy, and universe! Therefore, mankind was placed in a safe playpen, and 27 veils and limitations were placed upon the people of the Earth. It is now my great pleasure to share the 27 earthly plans, veils and limitations of GOD! Understanding what these are, I believe, will give each person a great insight into themselves and the nature of reality itself! For your pleasure and edification, here is the list of the 27 veils. After listing them, I will go into a short detailed description about each one!

1. The Veil of Reincarnation
2. The Veil of a Limited Lifespan
3. The Veil Between Species
4. The Veil of Limited Light, Thought, Feeling, Energy, and Power
5. The Veil of Aging
6. The Veil of Past Lives
7. The Veil of Remembrance
8. The Veil of Bondedness to the Physical Body
9. The Veil of the Ring-Pass-Not
10. The Veils of Time and Space
11. The Veil of Singular Dimensionality
12. The Veil of the Five Senses
13. The Veil of Prophecy and/or Seeing the Future
14. The Veil of Psychic Abilities
15. The Veil of the Three Lower Bodies
16. The Veil of the Limitation of Matter
17. The Veil of Karma

18. The Veil of the Prime Directive
19. The Veil of Mass Consciousness Programming
20. The Veil of Inner Sight
21. The Veil of Inner Hearing
22. The Veil of Inner Touch
23. The Veil of the Gifts of the Holy Spirit and Advanced Ascended Master Abilities
24. The Veil of the Kundalini
25. The Veil of God Realization
26. The Veil of Integrated Ascension
27. The Veil of God Realization

The Veil of Reincarnation

The plan that was set up by GOD and the Godforce to remedy this descent into forgetfulness and Spiritual sleep was "Reincarnation"! GOD and the Godforce created five races on the five continents of the Earth! A white, black, brown, yellow and red race! The different skin colors were not because one was better than another, but was because of the different climate conditions! The plan that was created was that all those souls who had fallen asleep would reincarnate over and over again until the seven levels of initiation were completed in a balanced and integrated manner so liberation from the wheel of rebirth and/or graduation would be achieved! The idea was that having time on the inner plane between lives would give souls time to remember who they were, and give them time to introspect and reflect before incarnating again!

The Veil of a Limited Lifespan

When this plan was instituted, there was a time when people could live on the Earth for 1000 years! The only problem was that Sons and Daughters of God were Spiritually sleeping for all 1000 years! So, GOD and the Godforce instituted a new veil and limitation. People could only live up to 125 years per lifetime so more time for introspection and self-reflection could be added into the process and so time on Earth was not wasted! This, of course, could be changed through the process of physical ascension, but this entails achieving Spiritual Realization first!

The Veil Between Species

Another adjustment, veil and limitation had to be set up later in the plan, for during the Atlantean period people would mate with animals, which created species that were part animal and part man! We are all aware of such creatures in our mythology. Some of these were real! GOD and the Godforce had to set up another veil and limitation that prevented inter-species reproduction!

The Veil of Limited Light, Thought, Feeling, Energy, and Power

One of the main veils and limitations that had to be set up by GOD and the Godforce was the profound decrease of light power, thought power, feeling power, and energy that Sons and Daughters of GOD were allowed to have! Where a Cosmic Being was allowed, for example, a billion watts of energy and light, on Earth mankind was given something like 100 watts and no more! Through the process of Spiritual evolution on all levels more could be attained, however, mankind's wattage in terms of its light power, mind power, emotional power and energetic power was greatly decreased until it proved worthy of using its energies in a non-misqualified manner!

Through the process of God Realization this could be greatly changed and increased, however, not until souls were deemed responsible to use this increase in light, love and power properly!

The Veil of Aging

As another part of this plan, a veil and limitation was set up in regard to the aging of the physical body! The soul, of course, is eternal and never ages! Part of the plan was that Sons and Daughters of GOD would have bodies that aged to foster the learning of lessons! This, of course, could be overcome through physical immortality and physical ascension, but God Realization would have to be achieved to do this!

The Veil of Past Lives

The next veil that God and the Godforce set up was a veil of forgetting all one's past lives! This was set in place because most Earthlings were so overwhelmed by the lessons of even one incarnation that it was deemed wise to prevent the remembering so as not to cause the incarnating soul to be overwhelmed with too many lessons and processing that they were ill-equipped to deal with!

The Veil of Remembrance

A similar type of veil was set up that Spirit calls the "Veil of Remembrance"! This veil not only extended to past lives but future lives, parallel lives, lives of one's 144 soul extensions from one's Monad, Extraterrestrial lifetimes, and memory of any time spent between life-times! This was done for the same reason as prevention of past life remembering! It was deemed that this would be too overwhelming to the incarnated soul. One incarnation was enough to handle! If God Realization was achieved, all this information could be retrieved in deeper layers of the subconscious mind and soul memory!

The Veil of Bondedness to the Physical Body

The next veil that was set up was a bonding of the soul to the physical body to prevent conscious soul travel! As we all know, when we leave the physical body we are free spirits and can travel anywhere we want in the infinite universe with the power of our mind! The second we think, we can travel there! Because of mankind's low state of consciousness, this had to be prevented on a conscious level so this was only allowed to occur when we slept! This added to the person's belief that they were a physical body, however, this could not be helped because of the misqualified energy that could be created if the soul was allowed to consciously roam the universe while being run by the negative ego. It was actually done as a self-protection as well! Through the process of Spiritual evolution, this ability could be consciously developed, but only when the soul was ready to use its energies in a more masterful, Spiritual and qualified manner!

The Veil of the Ring-Pass-Not

The veil of the ring-pass-not was placed around our planet like a kind of child's playpen, to prevent one from escaping and to prevent any negative energy from going out into the universe as well! It is like in a hospital wing where a certain section of the hospital is cordoned off. Another example might be a type of quarantine during an outbreak of a certain disease! A given area is quarantined to contain the energy! This was done to prevent any of the negative energy from all the people of the planet to spread around the solar system, galaxy, or universe! This would, of course, be lifted when mankind raised its consciousness to a level where it was no longer needed. Much like when a child grows up, much of the previous structures and rules are canceled because the child has matured and become responsible!

The Veils of Time and Space

The next veil that was placed by GOD and the Godforce is the veil of time and space. In the higher dimensions, there is no linear time! This, in truth, is an illusion of third-dimensional existence. In the higher dimensions, there is just the "eternal now"! This is why a person can view past and future lives! Why the future can be foretold to a large degree! In the higher planes, there is a process much like multidimensional existence! Space does not exist as it does in the First Heaven of GOD! It is much more of multidimensional reality! So, the veil of time and space and third-dimensional reality and linear time is built into this existence. Mankind added to this veil, however, by densifying matter, as I already described in the beginning of this chapter! Through the process of Spiritual evolution and meditation, the transcendence of time and space can be experienced and developed even while living in a physical body, however, not until self-mastery in a Spiritual sense is achieved to a certain degree!

The Veil of Singular Dimensionality

This next veil is connected a little bit with what I was speaking about in the last section! In truth, we are multidimensional beings existing on many planes of existence simultaneously. A veil was placed upon the Sons and Daughters of GOD to cause an identification with a "singular dimensionality," again as to not overwhelm the newly developing soul! Can you imagine if an undeveloped soul experienced all their multidimensional aspects? They would think they were schizophrenic! This is all veiled by the Love of GOD and the Godforce as a loving protection which can, of course, be opened up when one is ready through the process of God Realization and "Integrated Ascension"!

The Veil of the Five Senses

The next veil that was placed around us was the veil of the five senses. In truth, we have 22 "supersenses," which have often been called ESP or extra sensory perception! These other senses were veiled and limited by GOD and the Godforce! Can you imagine an unevolved soul who had all 22 supersenses of GOD wide open? They would be completely overwhelmed Spiritually, psychologically, and psychically! Hence, GOD and the Godforce placed a veil over these supersenses until the incarnated soul was ready to open up to them through the process of Spiritual evolution!

The Veil of Prophecy and/or Seeing the Future

The next veil that was placed upon mankind by GOD and the Godforce was the veil of prophecy or seeing the future! This is similar to the one in regard to past lives, but in reverse! You can again imagine how overwhelmed and fearful it would make an unevolved soul to have the ability to predict future events. There would be no context to fit this into, and they might see enormous numbers of future negative personal and collective events if they were run by negative thoughts on a personal and collective level. For this reason, a veil was placed over this ability as well! This can, however, be reopened through the process of achieving Spiritual development and Self-Realization!

The Veil of Psychic Abilities

The next veil that was set up by GOD and the Godforce was the veil over all psychic abilities. Now understand, my Beloved Readers, that the psychic realm is not a Spiritual realm. It is a subconscious realm. The subconscious mind has certain abilities that can be tapped into, and psychic abilities are one of them. The glamour of psychic abilities sidetracks many on the Spiritual path. Many psychics do not even believe in GOD! This is for the reasons I have stated! A veil was placed over these abilities as well, until people were seen as being evolved enough to use them properly. Even in this day and age, psychic abilities are often used for black magic, spells, omens, and negative forms of witchcraft or psychism. The abilities themselves, the perceptions they would bring, and their misuse was why this veil was placed upon the Sons and Daughters of GOD!

The Veil of the Three Lower Bodies

The next veil that was placed by GOD and the Godforce was the veil of the three lower bodies. Within each person's mind is a Higher Self or Oversoul, and above that the Mighty I Am Presence or Monad! The way it was set up is that the Higher Self did not pay much attention to the unconscious soul until it paid attention to the Higher Self! To achieve Spiritual Realization, the incarnated soul would have to build the Antakarana, or line of light, to the Higher Self and then back to the Mighty I Am Presence! When the soul achieved the Third Initiation the Higher Self, or Oversoul, would merge or blend its consciousness with the soul on Earth! At the Fourth Initiation, the Mighty I Am Presence would become the teacher for the incarnated soul instead of the Higher Self. At the Sixth Initiation, the Mighty I Am Presence and/or Monad would begin to merge with the incarnated soul on Earth! This culminates in the completion of the initial stages of ascension. Full GOD ascension, or Cosmic ascension, could not occur until all 352 initiations had been realized! It was set up that souls were not allowed to go to the next level until mastery, demonstration, and realization were achieved at the level they were at! This law applies through the planetary, solar, galactic, universal, and multiuniversal, all the way until the 352nd level of GOD is realized! This veil deals with the fact that incarnated souls must make an effort to connect with GOD with their own free choice before the Higher Self will even pay attention! Hence, I call this "The Veil of the Three Lower Bodies"! Even to this day, there are a great many souls on Earth who are completely disconnected from their Higher Self, Monad and GOD! All they believe in is their three lower bodies: mind, feelings, and physical body! They live under the illusion of the concrete mind and hence they have no connection to the higher mind or intuition! Hence, we have the atheist or the scientist who only believes in what the five senses tell them. The only thing that is real is what an experiment tells them! Then we have the person falling under the glamour of their emotional body thinking that all that is real is their feelings and emotions! Here we have the Humanistic Psychology Movement and/or people run by just the emotional body, astral body, and desire body! Thirdly and lastly, we have the Materialists, who believe in nothing but materialistic concerns. Hard to believe that people in this day and age 18.5 million years later in the evolutionary process could still be completely cut off from their Higher Self and any Spirituality; however, this is still very widespread on the Earth! Hence, "The Veil of the Three Lower Bodies"!

The Veil of Limitation of Matter

The next veil is that all beings must live under the auspices of the physical, mental, emotional, and etheric laws of this universe! Whenever souls get out of harmony with these laws, they cause their own suffering! The setting-up of these veils of limitation was to lovingly force souls to become obedient to GOD's Laws. If there were no laws, then souls would become unconscious for eternity and never change. What makes souls wake up is that in being disobedient to the laws they bring suffering upon themselves, which forces them to seek truth as a means to alleviate suffering! It is possible to transcend all physical laws! Sai Baba is a being who has transcended all physical laws! Jesus demonstrated this by being able to walk on water, turn water into wine, raise the dead, and so on! It is possible for all souls on Earth to transcend all physical laws through the process of God Realization and "Integrated Ascension"!

The Veil of Karma

The next veil and limitation that was placed was the law of karma. This law is that everything that a person puts out in thought, feeling, word and deed comes back to them, and this law extends over past lives! So, people may look like they are escaping, but no one ever does! This was the true meaning of the Biblical phrase, "Vengeance is mine sayeth the Lord"! As the Universal Mind said through Edgar Cayce, "Every jot and title of the law is fulfilled"! To achieve ascension and liberation at least 50% of one's karma must be cleansed and balanced; this is the system that was set up by GOD and the Godforce!

The Veil of the Prime Directive

I call this next veil, "The Veil of the Prime Directive"! This veil was that GOD and the Godforce were not allowed to help in any form unless asked! Sons and Daughters of GOD were given free choice, and this was not allowed to be interfered with. If the person did not ask, no help would be forthcoming from the Spiritual world! With one word of asking or praying, the force of Creation would come to serve and help!

The Veil of Mass Consciousness Programming

This veil deals with the fact that the way GOD and the Godforce have set up the Divine structure for the Earth and Sons and Daughters of GOD is to have them incarnate into babies' bodies. They are, of course, by nature, totally dependent and, in truth, total victims of parental, extended family and societal programming until they develop their reasoning mind and the Spiritual and psychological wisdom and knowledge to protect themselves. By the time this occurs, the person has become filled with "mass consciousness programming"! The only choice we have in this matter that GOD and the Godforce has given us is to be able to choose our parents from the inner plane. That does help a lot, however, this choice is also governed by the laws of karma and the availability of parents which, in truth, are not too available since they are in such high demand! So built into the system is a certain "mass consciousness veil" of personality level and negative ego programming that must be completely undone by the aspiring Spiritual Master! For this reason, I call this veil, "The Veil of Mass Consciousness Programming"!

The Veil of Inner Sight

This next veil that GOD and the Godforce put up was a veil to all inner sight of the inner planes of existence! This was to protect the unevolved souls from being completely overwhelmed and scared by all they would see! It was enough to deal with just the energies of this dimension that they could see! This inner sight, however, could be developed through the process of Spiritual evolution, both on a Spiritual and psychological level!

The Veil of Inner Hearing

The next veil is that of inner hearing! GOD and the Godforce also put up a veil to clairaudience, or the hearing of Spirits talking in the Spiritual world! This was done to protect unevolved souls. If they were hearing Spirits, their negative ego thinking would have them focused on the astral plane, and so the only Spirits they would hear would be lower astral ones. So, this faculty had to be veiled as well!

The Veil of Inner Touch

The next veil set up was that of clairsentience, or inner touch! It would be totally overwhelming to the unevolved soul to experience all these subtle energies! It was decided that this would be available to the soul only when they were at a high enough Spiritual and psychological level of development to handle it and know what to do with it!

The Veil of the Gifts of the Holy Spirit and Advanced Ascended Master Abilities

The next veil that was set up was the cutting off of all the gifts of the Holy Spirit and advanced Ascended Master abilities! With such an unevolved consciousness, these Spiritual powers or Siddhis as they are called in the East, would not be appropriate until mankind was at a level of consciousness, responsibility and development to use these abilities only for a Divine purpose and in a qualified way!

The Veil of the Kundalini

The next veil that was placed was a veil over the rising of the kundalini! This was done as a means of self-protection for the unevolved Sons and Daughters of GOD. We all know of stories about people who forced the raising of their kundalini prematurely and too rapidly and who suffered extreme damage on many levels. A veil was placed over this energy to not allow it to rise without Spiritual training! Kundalini should not be forced to rise. It should rise as a natural by-product of integrated Spiritual evolution!

The Veil of Integrated Ascension

The next veil that was established was that no soul would be allowed to take any initiations beyond the Seventh Initiation if they had not on some basic level integrated these initiations into their mental, emotional, physical, and Earthly selves! One of the Spiritual assignments the Masters have given me is to help lightworkers to do this; to remedy all the disintegration, fragmentation, glamour, maya and illusion that is currently manifesting in the New Age Movement and the world's religions! This area of my service work is my humble contribution to the healing of this lesson!

Any soul who does not master the psychological level, or mental and emotional level, will be forced to reincarnate again on the mental or emotional plane even if they have completed their seven levels of initiation. This will only occur if there is somewhat of a serious issue of nonintegration, victim consciousness, negative ego contamination and corruption or fragmentation. One does not have to be perfect to achieve full liberation; you just must be "in the ballpark," so to speak, of "Integrated Ascension"! Enormous numbers of people in the world's religions and in the New Age Movement are not even in the ballpark, and don't realize it. A number of my books, including *Integrated Ascension* and *How to Release Fear-Based Thinking and Feeling: An In-depth Study of Spiritual Psychology*, have been written to heal, remedy and correct these imbalances! Please tell your students, family and friends all about them, for there are not that many books on the market that really understand this level of the Spiritual path and can explain it in an easy to understand manner! Spirit and the Masters ask for your help, as do I, to spread this most important teaching, message and integrated Spiritual practice!

The Veil of God Realization

The last veil I call "The Veil of God Realization"! The purpose of life is to Realize God! This is not something GOD, however, will do for you! This is something you must do with your own personal power and free choice! All of Creation is going through this process. Even if we never ate of the fruit from the Tree of Good and Evil or thought a negative ego thought or feeling, we would still be going through the 352 levels of initiation! This was part of the Divine Plan of GOD, that all beings in GOD's Infinite Universe would not just be God because GOD created you, but would also go through this process of evolution to Realize God with their free choice! The eating of the fruit from the Tree of Good and Evil, and the corresponding densification of matter, made this process a little more complicated and a little more difficult, however this was in part our doing for this was not part of the plan! GOD and the Godforce in their infinite love and compassion set up these veils, limitations and restrictions to protect us, as I have described in this chapter, with the love and care of a most protective parent to insure that all souls who fell asleep would eventually wake-up! Thanks to noble beings like Sanat Kumara who came from Venus over 18.5 million years ago to become our Planetary Logos until souls on Earth could awaken enough to take control of their Spiritual government for themselves! We are by the Grace of GOD, Christ, and the Holy Spirit, at a time in the history of the Earth where this is now taking place! We are at the brink of moving into and realizing the seventh Golden Age for this planet!

It is my humble hope and prayer that this chapter has been helpful and enlightening for you to understand these 27 veils and restrictions and why they needed to be put into effect by GOD and the Godforce!

8

The Tree of Knowledge of Good and Evil and the Understanding of Polarity

The Biblical story of the Tree of Knowledge of good and evil is a most wonderful symbology and metaphor for understanding the negative ego and fear-based programming! In this Biblical story, Adam and Eve are told not to eat the apple of good and evil. In the story, Eve is tempted by the snake. The original plan of GOD's Creation was, of course, that we have free choice. The original Divine Plan, however, was that we would make choices within the realm of goodness without evil ever entering the picture.

Now, this brings up a very interesting discussion on the subject of Polarity and Duality. We all hear that part of the Spiritual Path is to "Transcend Duality"! This, in truth, would be the same as "Transcending negative ego thinking" and would also be the same as "Transcending evil." When we say Transcending Duality, this does not mean that there is no polarity. For even if Adam and Eve had never eaten the apple off the Tree of good and evil, there would still be polarity. There would still be

Feminine and Masculine, God/Goddess, Priest/Priestess, and/or Yin and Yang. It was never meant in GOD's Plan that we taste the apple; which is negative ego thinking, evil, judgement, or darkness! Once judgment enters, then things are labeled good and bad. One is a winner and one is a loser. Separation and fear enter the picture for the first time. Selfishness enters the picture. Anger enters in, and hurt, jealousy, envy, sadness, depression, upset and the entire gamut of negative feelings and emotions enters in.

My Beloved Readers, you will find this next understanding quite interesting. In Earth's history, when beings first incarnated on Earth over ten million years ago, the beings that first incarnated were more etheric in nature and were not physical as we are now. The planet and physical bodies looked like bodies, however, they were of a much lighter and refined nature, and matter was not dense as it is now. You will find it interesting to know that the densification of matter as it exists now was not part of GOD's Divine Plan. In the early Lemurian times it really was a Golden Age on this planet, and this was the "Eden" this Biblical story speaks of, although the story is also depicting psychological principles as well. In early Lemuria there was no separation. There was no veil between the Spiritual and Material world. There was no negative ego, separation, masculine and feminine imbalance, God/Goddess imbalance, evil, judgment, fear, selfishness, and all the rest. This was the first Golden Age on this planet. This was the Edenic state!

So, the key question is, "What happened?" It was when mankind ate the apple from the Tree of Good and Evil, or in other words, used their free choice to think with their negative ego mind instead of remaining in their Spiritual/Melchizedek/Christ/Buddha mind, that fear, separation, and all the negative feelings and emotions began to be created. This was as the Biblical story tells, the "Banishment from Eden"! Eden being both the Spiritual/Christ/Buddha consciousness and also early Lemuria and the first Golden Age on this planet! It was in misusing our free choice and choosing to think with our negative ego/fear-based/separative mind that not only caused all the negative feelings and emotions, it is also what caused then the densification of matter both on the Earth and within our physical bodies. I emphasize again that this was never part of GOD's Divine Plan. It was never meant for people to suffer or for the veils to be so dense. Even death of the physical body was not part of the Divine Plan. It was only after densification took place and people were getting lost in separation and the density of matter that the plan of reincarnation was developed. This was an afterthought; otherwise, people would be lost in matter forever. Death of the physical body allowed a time on the inner plane for Spiritual reflection and review before continuing the process again.

It was only because of this choice of misusing free choice, eating the apple, and choosing negative ego thinking instead of God thinking, that feminine and masculine energies became imbalanced. It was because of this that God/Goddess became imbalanced and the Patriarchy took over. It was because of this that the veils between the Spiritual and Material world became so severe. It was because of this that people got cut off from their Higher Self and Mighty I Am Presence within their consciousness. It was because of this that war and conflict began! It was because of this that all negative feelings and emotions began. It was because of this that the Patriarchy took over and the Divine Mother/Goddess energies and the Matriarchy were rejected. It was because of this that all selfishness began. It was why roses grew thorns! It was the cause of the abuse of the Earth Mother and the getting cut off from the Nature Kingdom. It was because of this that people began closing down their feelings and emotions because they didn't want to feel any more pain or suffering. It was because of this choice that the people got cut off from the Ascended Masters, Angels, and Elohim! It is because of this choice that we became disconnected from the Elemental Kingdom and Devas of the Earth. It was this choice that caused the entire Earth and our physical bodies to densify to such a degree. It was this choice that caused Spirit and the Masters to develop the plan of reincarnation! None of this would have ever occurred if this choice had not been made. Now do understand that even if Adam and even if mankind had never eaten of the Tree of Good and Evil there still would be an evolutionary process and there still would be the 352 levels of initiation. For this was all part of GOD's Plan, which is quite interesting! However, all choices would be made in the realm of only the "Good" or only within "GOD" or only within the "Spiritual/Christ/Buddha consciousness"!

Darkness was never meant to be part of GOD's Divine Plan. Glamour, illusion and maya were all a product of this choice! The snake was on a psychological level—the negative ego or fear-based mind.

This choice ultimately led to the destruction of Lemuria in catastrophic Earth changes. The continent of Atlantis was later destroyed for the same reason. It was a technologically advanced civilization, and Spiritually advanced in many ways as well, however, the contagion of negative ego took over a great many leaders and scientists of the planet and they destroyed Atlantis and it sank to the bottom of the ocean in a series of Earth changes over many thousands of years.

The Earth was not meant to be such a difficult Spiritual school that it has become! This was not GOD and the Masters' doing; this was the misuse of free choice by mankind! Now from GOD and the Masters' perspective there is no judgment in what has occurred. It is just that the evolutionary process and initiation process was supposed to occur only in the realm of "Goodness"! Choices would be made in the realm of polarity, however, only in the context of "Goodness"! Many adjustments have been made in the Divine Plan out of GOD's great love for his Sons and Daughters to try and rectify this situation. Sanat Kumara and his 144 Kumaras were sent in the earliest of times to save this Beloved Planet and bring it back into Light! No one is judged for what happened, for maybe, in truth, from another perspective it was inevitable given that we had been given free choice. We also must consider that we are not the only planet that deals with this issue. All of Creation does! This is not to say that all planets have made the same choices, for they have not. Maldek was a planet that actually destroyed itself for the choices it made! Some have associated the snake in this Biblical story to the negative Extraterrestrials, like the Grays or Reptilian race. This may not be completely inaccurate as well!

The good news is that after 18.5 million years we are now returning to another Golden Age on this planet! It is now time for the Divine Mother and Goddess energies to return! It is now time for the rebalancing of the Three-Fold Flame within the hearts of all the people of the Earth! It is now the time for the Earth Mother to be healed and for the stopping of the abuse that mankind has repeated upon her! By the Grace of GOD and the Masters this time has now come! To achieve this, however, we each must become an "Integrated Melchizedek/Christ/Buddha" in our daily lives! We must each achieve "Integrated Ascension"! It is then that we can return to the "Garden of Eden" within our own Spiritual/Melchizedek/Christ/Buddha consciousness and this will then be reflected on the Earth as well.

So be of good cheer, for the Earth has entered the very beginning of this Golden Age where this will take place. Over the next 25 years, we will see the most rapid period of Spiritual and Psychological growth in the history of this planet! It is in returning to this "Garden of Eden consciousness" that we can transcend all evil, all darkness, all separation, all fear, negative ego, and all negative selfishness, negative feelings and emotions. It is then that we can transcend negative ego duality. For as Krishna taught Arjuna in the *Bhagavad-Gita*—it is possible to live in a transcended state of consciousness that transcends negative ego duality and remains even-minded at all times even in the face of profit or loss, pleasure or pain, sickness or health, and victory or defeat. Whether people criticize you or praise you, you remain the same! This state of consciousness is possible when you learn to think with your Spiritual/Christ/Buddha mind instead of your negative ego/fear-based/separative mind! For if you notice, all dualities I mentioned are outside of self. Since we each cause our own reality by how we think, it is possible to develop a way of thinking that allows us to remain in unconditional love, forgiveness, nonjudgmentalness, even-mindness, joy, happiness, preference, non-attachment, harmlessness, defenselessness, gentleness, patience, faith, and to look at everything as a

Spiritual test and Spiritual lesson at all times. This is possible because things outside of self do not cause us to think or feel anything. It is our interpretation, belief system and perception of what goes on outside of ourself that causes us to feel the way we do. This is because our thoughts cause our feelings. Outside things or people don't cause us to feel what we do, our thoughts do. We can't always control what comes to us from the outside world; however, we can control the attitude and interpretation we take towards the things that happen, which is the key. There are only two philosophies of life, the negative ego/fear-based/separative way of thinking or the Spiritual/Melchizedek/Christ/Buddha way of thinking. Which attitude and philosophy we take will determine how we feel any given moment! Does not the Bible say, "Let this Mind be in you that was in Christ Jesus"? The name of it does not matter. If you want to call it the Melchizedek Mind, the Buddha Mind, the Spiritual Mind, the Christ Mind, God Mind, or just your Positive Mind, it is fine. GOD does not care and neither do the Masters, for it is all the same thing! It is in choosing this way of thinking and interpreting life that will bring the "Peace that Passeth Understanding"! It will also allow you to learn your Spiritual lessons, graduate, achieve liberation, and remain on Earth to serve and demonstrate the Glory of GOD and unconditional love within the perfect balance of the Three-Fold Flame of GOD of Love, Wisdom and Power! It is when these three Divine qualities are perfectly balanced and integrated that God Realization is most perfectly demonstrated!

So be of good cheer, for the "Garden of Eden consciousness" is now upon you, and our world has now begun the first initial steps of entering the Seventh Golden Age and the return of the "Garden of Eden" physically to this world! There is still much to do, and it is each of our Spiritual Missions to play our part within GOD's Divine Plan! This is a most auspicious time to be incarnated on this Earth! Count your blessings, for souls are lining up on the inner plane trying to enter this glorious time of accelerated Spiritual and psychological growth on this planet! This information being brought forth has Melchizedek, the inner plane Cosmic and

Planetary Hierarchy, and myself in a Co-Creative effort to help every Spiritual leader, lightworker, and this planet accelerate this process on a Spiritual, Psychological and Physical/Earthly Level, and in an integrated and balanced way!

9

The In-Breath and Out-Breath of Brahma

There is a cosmic event that is about to happen to Planet Earth and the cosmos as a whole that almost defies description. We are very, very close to the middle of a cosmic cycle, soon to reach the exact midpoint between the out-breath and in-breath of God.

Many people might not realize that just as humans on Earth breathe, so does God. Djwhal Khul has said that the process of breathing occurs even after the Ascended Master state of consciousness is reached. God breathes out creation and then breathes it back in again.

The out-breath and in-breath of God could be likened to the swing of a pendulum. As the pendulum swing reaches its uppermost apex, there is a moment of complete rest before it continues its movement in the opposite direction. This moment of rest and lack of movement in God's breathing is a moment of non-time, of eternity. Since the microcosm is like the macrocosm, this same process occurs many times each second as atoms of the physical world vibrate back and forth.

In the meditations of Sai Baba, Paramahansa Yogananda, and Baba Muktananda, the mantra "So Hum" or "So Ham" or "Hong Sau" are used.

These mantras mean "I Am God" or "I Am the Self," and are actually the sound of humans breathing as God listens. The idea of this meditation is to say the mantra in accordance with the breath. The main idea of the meditation is to listen to the "stillpoint," or point of eternity, between the in-breath and out-breath as we say the mantra. This point of null time is a doorway into the presence of God.

Just as we have the opportunity to experience this at any time if we choose to tune in to it at the moment between our own breaths, we also have the most unbelievably profound opportunity to listen to this stillpoint between God's in-breath and out-breath, which occurs, according to Vywamus, only every ten million years in Earth's time. The exact moment between the expanding and contracting of the entire cosmos coincides, by no accident, with the Second Coming of Christ and the end of the Mayan calendar.

This exact midpoint between the in-breath and out-breath of God (Brahma) will occur in 2012. It will provide an opening for the emergence of something incomprehensible. In this moment, God will have the opportunity to slip into His creation. All materializing processes will become suspended.

This event will not be experienced simultaneously in all parts of the universe but will travel as a wave across the sea of Creation. Existing within this moment of non-time will be the focused, conscious attention of the Creator. The Archangel Raphael, in *The Starseed Transmissions* by Ken Carey, has predicted the year 2012 as its most exact point of focus for Planet Earth. Archangel Raphael has said that no single conceptual structure is capable of conveying the enormity of what is soon to take place.

In that moment we will experience ourselves as the Christ, the Atma, the Buddha, the Eternal Self. We will recognize the unified collective consciousness of all humankind as our own true identity. We will fully realize our identity as God defines us, rather than as matter and the negative ego define us. We will recognize ourselves as one conscious being expressing itself through a multitude of separate forms. This will initiate the second period of planetary awakening, which has been called the millennium or the one-thousand-year cycle.

In this future state, we will be able to live in two realities simultaneously—half the time in form and half the time in the totality of All That Is. We will truly see ourselves as the bridge between Spirit and Matter and as the means through which the Creator relates to His creation. It is in this period that the fictitious identity of ego, with its sense of separation, fear, and selfishness, will be transcended.

Djwhal Khul has referred to this shift from the out-breath to the in-breath of God as the completion of a Cosmic Day. The profundity of this can be seen in the fact that ten million years is the total amount of time humankind has been on Earth. In this shift we will release our identification with the past, with the future, and with our material bodies and begin to live more in the present moment. We will see our true mission to be expressing God on Earth. In the future, we will no longer be a random note in the symphony of God, but rather totally unified with the music of the spheres. None of us will consider ourselves better or worse than anyone else, for everyone will share the same identity as the Christ, as God. Christ is the single unified being whose consciousness we all share.

As we begin to play our individual note in attunement with the great conductor God, we will play in rhythm and in harmony with the planetary symphony. We will play our note in harmony with all other humans, animals, plants and minerals on Earth.

What has been happening is that we have each been playing our own negatively egotistical, selfish note that has made the symphony sound very discordant. This is about to change. None of us will ever again have to act superior out of imagined importance and put others down, because the truth of our real identity as the Christ is far beyond anything the negative ego could dream up. The Spirit and Soul recognize that all are of supreme importance equally.

In the new millennium we will all communicate in the universal language of Light. This form of communication is far more specific and inclusive than words or even telepathic communication. The living language of Light is the true universal language of God. The new millennium will bring back the pre-fall state of awareness that, in truth, never left. We just think it did. We have been rethinking this illusion that is programmed into us by our society—every morning when we wake up from our dreams and get out of bed. It can be changed any moment we choose to change it.

As we move through this final twenty-year cycle of the Mayan calendar, slowly but surely a critical mass of awakened and enlightened people will emerge. This will cause a "hundredth-monkey effect" and instantaneously transform humanity as a whole. This is a transformation from self-centeredness to God-centeredness.

This process, in truth, is as simple as where we put our attention. If we put our attention on our imagined negative ego identity, then that is where we will live. If we put our attention on our God-self identity, then we have awakened to the truth of our being. So many of us do not control the focus of our attention and operate on automatic pilot. That is our downfall. So, in truth, we live in two states of consciousness simultaneously. We are large enough to encompass all of Creation and yet, with our attention, can make ourselves small enough to climb inside of Creation into a physical body. The problem is that the negative ego tells us that all we are is the body. In the God-realized state, we oscillate between the two as circumstance and our mission require. There is an appropriate movement from the totality of being to form, and back again. In the God-realized state, even though our attention has moved back to our form identity, we still retain our awareness of our oneness with and identity in God. The God-realized state allows both states of consciousness, whereas the negative ego tells us that all that exists is our form identity.

In the new millennium there will be a return to ecological balance and international cooperation, including an end to war. We will all seek to realize God's Divine plan instead of our own. We will become the means through which God will implement His will in the realm of form.

Awakening from the Spell of Matter

In this new millennium, humanity as a whole will wake up from the spell of matter. This planet is a seventh-dimensional planet; however, in the past we have been perceiving it as a three-dimensional planet. From the perspective of Spirit and the Angels, we have had some strange, debilitating perceptual disorder. We have identified with form rather than with essence. We have identified ourselves with temporal time rather than with eternity. We have identified ourselves with the visible rather than with the invisible. We have been living in a negative hypnosis.

The challenge of the New Age is to retain our human forms and yet awaken from this hypnosis. According to Archangel Raphael in *The Starseed Transmissions* by Ken Carey, the angels have been programmed to awaken us at a certain point in history. This point was reached at the birth of Jesus Christ. He has described himself as the way we were, are now, and will be after the spell of matter is broken. It has taken the angels two thousand years to prepare us en masse for the profound transformation that is about to take place—fully moving us into the New Age.

The Ego and the Spirit

In coming to a proper understanding of this whole process I would like to discuss an understanding of the ego different from the one I have previously given. Previously, I have defined ego as the attitude system that is the opposite of the Christ consciousness; the attitude system that is based on the premise that we are physical bodies rather than Spirit living in physical bodies. This illusion leads to the illusionary belief in separation, fear, selfishness, and so on.

I am purposely putting into this chapter a semantically different understanding of the term "ego" because it is a dilemma that all disciples on the path are running into in their studies. Half the schools of thought use the term "ego" as Sai Baba does when be says that "God equals man minus ego." The other half of the schools of thought use it in another way, which I would like to explain now, for it is probably a better understanding of the process.

The "ego," in this new understanding, is the valid and most important part of self that gives us a sense of identity and individuality. It helps us to function in this world and to complete our missions here. Having an ego goes along with having a physical body.

The ego's true function is to be a retriever of information and to remind the soul extension who is living in the body to take care of its physical body. The ego prevents the soul extension from doing something that would prove damaging to the physical vehicle. The ego is the material plane expert. If we didn't have an ego, we might forget that we are even incarnated. So the ego reminds us that we need water, food, and sleep.

Now, the problem arises because the ego was never meant to interpret the rest of our lives for us. The rest of our lives were meant to be defined and interpreted by the Soul and Spirit. We have let the ego interpret our reality. The ego's interpretation is based on the faulty belief that we are bodies (because that is all it knows about), and we have let the ego override intuitive ways of processing information of the Spirit. The Spirit's right-brained method of processing information using intuition, higher mind, spiritual will, and other faculties, can process information instantaneously. In interpreting our realities, the ego has misused the conscious, reasoning mind and created an illusionary belief system based on fear, separation, selfishness, and death.

It has also overridden and blocked out the superior, computer-like circuitry of the Spirit's primary information system. The ego, at best, can use only 10% of the brain. It is only when the Spirit's information processing system is used that the potential of using 100% of the brain can be tapped.

When the fall occurred, humankind as a whole shifted to the ego's cumbersome and illusionary manner of interpreting. The ideal would have been to balance the ego's and the Spirit's functions in the proper manner. I emphasize that the ego was never meant to interpret our reality, only to be a retriever of information and to be the resident expert on the physical body. To interpret reality through the ego is to interpret reality through the physical eyes only. We have not allowed the ego to become Spiritualized; it has become a *negative* ego. When Sai Baba and other teachers say we should die to our egos, what they are really saying is we must die to the negative ego, or Spiritualize the ego. Both schools of thought are totally valid. It is just a semantics issue.

In the ideal state the Spirit and ego work in perfect balance, and we live in two worlds simultaneously. This will be the prototype individual in the new millennium.

The New Millennium

The next twenty years will see the most rapid period of change human civilization has ever known. We have already seen this happening in the fall of Communism in the Soviet Union and East Germany. There have been many predictions by many psychics and prophets of both ancient and modern times of a coming shifting of the axis of the Earth.

There will be no physical shifting of the poles, based on the information I have received. It is not that this information was wrong when it was prophesied, but rather that humankind has changed enough that the shift doesn't need to happen in this way. The true axis shift will occur in consciousness. It will be a shift from negative ego thinking to Spiritual- or Christ-thinking on a mass scale. It will not need to happen in the physical because it is beginning to happen in consciousness.

If things seem to be moving fast now, we can only imagine how fast things will seem to move when the Soul and Spirit are allowed to interpret our reality in proper relationship to the ego function, as God would have it. When this happens, we will be using the other 90% of our brains to process information. In truth, we are still living in the dark ages, or like cave men, compared to what it will be like when we are utilizing the lightning-like ways of the Spirit to process information. All new technologies will no longer be based on limited egotistical and materialistic thinking. The technologies of the future will all be environmentally helpful, not hurtful. They will also be based on the ability to transcend time, space, and gravity. The Earth Mother is about to give birth to a New Age and we are just leaving our adolescence. In truth, our egos are relieved to be able to give up culturally induced responsibilities that they were never meant to take on. They can release this burden at any moment and not wait until 2012. It is as simple as letting go of a faulty belief and replacing it with a balanced one.

Each of us has a type of etheric antenna that connects us to the guidance of Soul and Spirit. The etheric antenna becomes disconnected from this higher guidance when we indulge in anger, hatred, and fear. It is not endangered by outside emotions, only by our own emotions. As long as we don't take on the negative vibrations and emotions of others, letting them slide off the golden bubble that is our shield, we are fine. It is also essential to learn to remain calm, peaceful, even-minded, and, most of all, loving and forgiving.

By learning to transcend the negative ego in this way, we remain connected to the etheric antenna and superior spiritual guidance. When we lose this attunement, we should just stop, forgive ourselves, try to learn the lesson, attitudinally heal ourselves, and ask ourselves whether we want God or our negative ego in that situation. By constantly choosing God rather than negative ego, over and over again, a habit will develop over time of not losing our etheric antenna's full sensitivities and attunement.

The Year 2012: A Quantum Leap in Consciousness

At the exact moment between the in-breath and out-breath of God there will be a massive change in the world that has no historical precedent on Planet Earth. Everything in Earth's gravitational field will be affected. There will be a mass awakening to the interconnectedness of all life. More energy will be released in those few moments than is normally released in many years. We will experience heightened perception and an emotional connection to God.

Each of us will experience these moments of non-time between the out-breath and in-breath of God differently. Some will experience them as minutes, some as hours, some as a lifetime, some as many lifetimes. Some of us may have a revelation of God while others will react in fear; depending on our state of consciousness. Some may choose to leave the physical body in that moment and return to the spiritual world. There will be a shift on a mass scale from fear to love, from outer-directedness to inner-directedness. We all will feel a surge of power. How this is interpreted, again, depends on our state of consciousness.

Archangel Raphael, in Ken Carey's *The Starseed Transmissions,* has said that there could be Earth changes, but not on the scale once predicted. The media may react in fear, and it is important that we not buy into their glamour, illusion, and maya, for this is not a fearful event, but a glorious, joyous, and wonderful event. In truth, it is something that we can experience at any moment if we listen to the null time, the eternity between our own breaths, for the microcosm is like the macrocosm, and we are made in God's image. However, this event will be occurring on a mass level, not just on an individual level. It could be said that we will be having a global meditation on God.

It is time for us to realize that as humanity we are the oak tree and no longer the acorn. In the future, the ego and Spirit will work in harmony much like the specific parts of a cell work in harmony. Just as we normally don't analyze the parts of a cell to see if it is functioning properly, so will ego and Spirit function as a whole. Each of us is a cell in the body of God. When ego and Spirit are integrated, then each of us will be a healthy cell in God's body.

We are living in an astonishing period of history. After ten million years, humanity is about to fully awaken. It is a great blessing to be incarnated at this time in Earth's history, for there has never been anything like it in terms of spiritual growth. Our work over the coming years is to prepare ourselves and others for the reappearance of the Christ, the externalization of the Hierarchy, and this coming quantum leap in consciousness.

The ideal would be to get all soul extensions to this Christ consciousness before these events even occur so we may move into the new Golden Age in total grace and love with no fear or karma. We have our work cut out for us during this last twenty-year cycle of the Mayan calendar. Lord Maitreya has said that he will not declare himself, and the full manifestation of the externalized Spiritual Hierarchy will not occur, until humankind is ready. The more work we can do on ourselves to realize the Christ and God within ourselves and within others, the sooner we will be catapulted into the New Age.

We on Earth at this time who are aware of these things are in a sense like God's infantry, an army of lightworkers laying the groundwork for our leader, the Christ, the Lord Maitreya. The only way he can succeed is if we help him, for his work and ours is to reawaken the Christ, the Buddha, the Atma, the Eternal Self, in all soul extensions on Earth.

The more awakened humanity is by the year 2012, the more powerful will be this moment of mass enlightenment. The combination of Lord Maitreya's coming, the externalization of the Hierarchy; the presence of Sai Baba, the Cosmic Christ.; the work of the Angels, the work of the Christed Extraterrestrial groups, and last but not least, the work of all the Masters and the New Group of World Servers already on Earth, cannot fail.

Our challenge is to become steadfast and focused in our personal work and in our service work, as we have never been before. We are each and every one cells in the body of God, and God will not be healthy until each and every one of us has realized our oneness and potential in Him. It is time to be born again to our true identity as the Christ and as one unified being. It is time to see all people as equals, regardless of their state of spiritual development or lack thereof. It is time to be about the Father's business, for His identity is, in truth, our identity. His purpose is our purpose. There is only one being in the infinite universe and that is God. He is incarnated in every mineral, plant, animal, human, planet, star, and galaxy.

In the future, all kingdoms will be looked at as equals. We are not superior to a flower, a cat, a dog, a crystal, or a rock. Each is a specific incarnation of God, with a specific purpose, mission, and attribute of God's infinite nature to express. As we transcend our negative egos, we will realize our proper place in the scheme of all life that is God.

10

The Seven Paths to Higher Evolution

At the time of taking your sixth initiation and ascension, you must make a decision as to which of the seven paths of higher evolution you will follow. As I have stated previously, the completion of the seven levels of initiation means that you are, in truth, only one inch up a ten-inch ruler, with nine inches to go. At that point you have completed the seven sub-planes of the cosmic physical plane but have not yet even entered the cosmic astral plane, the cosmic mental plane, the cosmic Buddhic plane, the cosmic atmic plane, the cosmic monadic plane, or the cosmic logoic plane.

One of the seven paths to higher evolution will serve as a focus on your journey. God is too infinitely vast for you to evolve without some kind of focus. All seven paths ultimately lead to the same place; even so, if you want to, it is possible to transfer from one path to another at a later time.

The Path to Sirius seems to serve as a preliminary training ground for some of the other paths that are more advanced. You must go on record as to which path you choose at the time of your ascension. It is a good idea to familiarize yourself with these seven paths now, even before you ascend, and to begin meditating upon them. The seven paths are the following:

1. The Path of Earth Service
2. The Path of Magnetic Work
3. The Path of Training to Become a Planetary Logos
4. The Path to Sirius
5. The Ray Path
6. The Path on which the Solar Logos Himself is Found
7. The Path of Absolute Sonship

I believe that Djwhal Khul, in his writings through Alice Bailey (particularly *Initiation, Human and Solar*), is the only Ascended Master who has ever written about these paths in any detail on the Earth plane. He has done humanity a tremendous service by doing so. The only problem is that some of the material is very technical and esoteric and difficult for the average person to understand.

With Djwhal's blessing I have attempted to expand upon his writings to make the information a little easier to understand and a little more accessible by humanity. It has taken a good deal of spiritual research to do this, and I consider this particular project one of the most important I have ever been involved with. It is my prayer that my efforts in this regard will be of value to you.

One: The Path of Earth Service

The Path of Earth Service is the first of the seven paths to higher evolution. If you choose this path, you remain on Earth or in the ashram of one of the seven chohans serving humanity from the inner plane. If you choose this path, you must also choose which kingdom (human, animal, plant, or mineral) to focus on based on which would profit the most from your abilities.

You can serve directly by incarnating, or indirectly from the spiritual world. The basic goal of this path is to raise the consciousness, frequency, level of love, and initiatory status of humanity and all the other kingdoms. All who choose this path work under Lord Buddha, the Planetary Logos.

There is also the issue here of choosing the Path of Earth Service on a temporary basis. I, for example, have chosen the Path to Sirius, but I have been told by Djwhal Khul that even though this is the case, I will be spending a period of time after leaving this physical body, in Djwhal's ashram working with him, much as we are working together now. Djwhal Khul has chosen the Path to Sirius. The interesting thing, however, is that Sanat Kumara has asked Djwhal to remain with the Earth and on the Path of Earth Service during this critical time in Earth's history. In a sense, you might say that Sanat Kumara chose the Path of Earth Service for Djwhal and Djwhal graciously agreed. However, he does a lot of training and work all over the universe in conjunction with this mission. Most people, after ascension and leaving the physical vehicle, will spend some time in Earth service from the inner plane as part of their training.

The Path of Earth Service deals with initiations seven through twelve, which take you up through the galactic level. After the ninth initiation you usually leave the cosmic physical universe altogether.

The Path of Earth Service, during this particular phase of Earth's development, is a most spectacular path because of the incredible speeding up of evolution that is taking place at this time. Earth will make more progress in the forty-year period from 1988 to 2028 than it has in the past 3.2 billion years. This path has been less popular in the past than, for example, the Path to Sirius.

Also, there has been a limit on the number of people who have been allowed to choose this path, and it has become more popular in the past fifty years. The Path of Earth Service is more familiar than any of the other six paths to higher evolution because, of course, it is the plane on which humans are incarnated. In a sense, all are on the Path of Earth Service and have been so for a very long time. The difference between that and what I am referring to in this chapter is that after the sixth initiation and ascension, when a path has been chosen, you serve with full self-realization.

As you remember, there are seven cosmic planes. The seven planes through which humans are evolving are only the seven sub-planes of the cosmic physical plane. The Path of Earth Service leads to the cosmic astral plane, as does the Path to Sirius. Some of the later paths lead to the cosmic mental plane and one even leads to the cosmic Buddhic plane.

Buddha, after his ascension, chose the Path of Earth Service. Interestingly enough, he realized later he had made a mistake and Sanat Kumara allowed him to choose the Path to Sirius. Lord Maitreya will soon do the same when his final mission here, during this millennium, is over. The Master Kuthumi will take over the position of the Planetary Christ.

The Path of Earth Service is the only path Sanat Kumara retains the right to, in a sense, draft new ascended masters onto. This, in truth, is a great honor and compliment, for he is saying your great skills and abilities are needed here. In such a case, these masters postpone their movement to one of the other paths, although their decisions are recorded. At a later time, in his omniscience, Sanat Kumara will notify them when it is time to leave.

Lord Maitreya will return to Earth at a much later time as the Cosmic Christ, which will be a great event in Earth's evolutionary history. The masters on the Path of Earth Service are working in conscious receptivity to the cosmic astral plane even before graduating to that level because the cosmic astral plane is the true source of the energy of love.

All seven paths lead either to the cosmic astral plane or to the cosmic mental plane. The cosmic astral plane is the Heart of God and the center of pure love. The cosmic mental plane is the plane of the Divine Mind. The cosmic Buddhic plane is the cosmic level of Pure Reason. All paths eventually lead to the Great Central Sun.

Much training occurs on the inner plane once you have chosen your path. Vywamus told me that there are classes in telepathy, in how to channel (both as a giver and as a receiver), in the science of impression (conveying your will and intent to your manifested body), and in direct Light transmission. There are classes in cyclic evolution that focus on the developmental stages of Earth's history, just as a class on Earth might chart the developmental stages of a baby. The incarnations of the great masters are evidence of key transition points within this developmental model.

Another class involves the study of various planets and their processes of coming into being, looking specifically at Earth's movement from the ideal etheric blueprint into a manifested state. The Earth-school model is, of course, not the only model for planetary evolution in this universe. There are many, many models; in fact, Earth is unique in its usage of emotion for spiritual development.

The Path of Earth Service is one of great teaching, both as a master and as a student, for there is always another level to unfold and another initiation toward which you are moving. The process is not complete until you move through all three hundred fifty-two levels of the Mahatma, so there is a long way to go.

The amount of time spent on the Path of Earth Service varies with each individual and with what is going on in the divine plan of Sanat Kumara. Many classes are developed on a spontaneous basis as the need arises. For example, this period of Earth's history has brought up many unique issues that past phases of Earth's history have never had to deal with.

Two: The Path of Magnetic Work

The Path of Magnetic Work is the second of the seven paths to higher evolution. If you choose this path, you learn to work with "fohat," the essential energy of the solar system, of the Solar Logos, Helios. Fohat energy is differentiated into seven major types. It is specifically with the astral energy of this planet and later of the solar system that you work, if you choose this path. You learn to direct the fohat energy into the Planetary astral plane to help clear the man-made glamour and delusion. The pure astral energy used on this path is free of delusion, for it is made up of pure unconditional love. On this path, you wield the force of this electrical magnetism under the direction of the Great Ones. Matter of every density and vibration is manipulated in service of the Divine Plan.

On this path, you also learn to work with the great waves of ideas and currents of public opinion on a planetary level. You learn to work with pure solar astral energy, pure galactic astral energy, and later, pure cosmic astral energy. If you choose this path, you must be trained to be an expert in timing and energy manipulation. The pure astral energy, or love energy, that is coming from the higher levels is also expressed as Light and Good Will. It is distributed to the Hierarchy as well as to humanity.

The Path of Magnetic Work first takes the master to the heart of the Sun and work with Helios and then to the cosmic mental plane, pausing only temporarily on the cosmic astral plane. It is through the use of magnetism that the planetary astral body is cleared, hence clearing humanity's consciousness. Djwhal Khul has stated that many initiates who have achieved liberation on the fifth ray, the ray of concrete knowledge, seem to follow this path of magnetic work.

Vywamus has told me that masters who choose this path deal with the concept of polarity balance on a planetary, solar, galactic, universal, and cosmic level, and also on a subatomic level. Working with magnetism involves balancing the universal forces. Much work is also focused on the grid lines of the Earth. The Path of Magnetic Work is a cosmic science that applies to creation on many levels. At its highest level it deals with the creation of universes, white holes, black holes, and star polarities. For human purposes, magnetics is focused on a planetary and solar level and is concerned with the evolving consciousness in incarnation.

The first training, Vywamus said, would be an observation class in which you observe how magnetic work is implemented in the cosmic plan. At the second step, you are allowed to experience the magnetic effect on a limited basis. The third step involves the application of magnetics in service to the planet.

An example of the observation phase might be the monitoring of a pulsation coming to Earth from the Galactic Core. The pulsation will cause an electromagnetic change. The master on this path develops great expertise in understanding and working with the effects of these electromagnetic adjustments on personal, planetary, solar, and galactic levels. He also develops an understanding of the relationship between energy and thought and between magnetics and polarity. Magnetics is applied on all levels primarily to maintain unity.

Magnetism is occurring all the time on Earth. There is emotional magnetism that occurs between a man and a woman who are in a romantic relationship. There is magnetism between any two people who are having an intellectual conversation. There is magnetism between any two people who are physically touching each other, for energy is being transferred. You already have some understanding of magnetism and you utilize that understanding in your daily life. The master who chooses the Path of Magnetic Work builds on this understanding in order to deal with humanity as a whole, with the planetary body and solar system, and later with the galaxy and cosmos themselves.

The master choosing this path learns the science of changing mass consciousness and public opinion through the dissemination of electromagnetic pulses and electromagnetic waves of energy. For example, one of the waves or pulses might be connected to the thoughtform of peace. Rays, colors, and sounds can be used in this way as well. It is on the astral plane, however, that most of this work is being done.

Ascended Masters do not operate out of the astral plane because for Earth it is the plane of delusion. By clearing and purifying the astral plane, they allow humankind to see reality more clearly, for then it is not living in a dark cloud of planetary delusion. It is hard to free yourself from this delusion on a personal level when the entire planet is one massive emotional fog. In this context, the importance of such work can be seen. I have often asked the Ascended Masters to magnetically pull all the etheric mucus out of my field if I am feeling unclear. Masters such as Lenduce or Vywamus can pull clouded energy right out of your field like a vacuum cleaner.

The astral-plane delusion around the planet could be likened to emotional smog. The masters on this path, using pure astral energy and the science of magnetics, clear the smog away and then influence consciousness on a planetary level toward the spiritual ideal. Vywamus told me that magnetics is used on all seven of the paths to higher evolution. In truth, it is the foundation for all other paths. Djwhal confirmed this also when he said it was one of the first paths to be tread upon after the evolutionary process was set in motion by Sanat Kumara.

Ten percent of humanity chooses this path as opposed to the other seven paths to higher evolution. Vywamus said that the science of magnetics could be described as the "understanding of the way to keep creation together in manifestation." It is to this larger ideal that the masters who have chosen this ideal work on all levels of God's creation.

Three: The Path of Training to Become a Planetary Logos

The Path of Training to Become a Planetary Logos is the third of the seven paths to higher evolution. It is the path that Sanat Kumara, Earth's Planetary Logos, has chosen. The masters choosing this path at their sixth initiation are being trained to take up the work of the seven planetary logoi and the forty-nine sub-planetary logoi and their assistants, for the next system. Each of the seven chohans, or lords, of the seven rays takes on a certain number of students and trains them specifically for this work. The masters choosing this path have a special aptitude for dealing with the psyche and are, hence, considered the divine or cosmic psychologists.

They also have a special aptitude for dealing with color and sound. Every planetary logos has his or her own planet and school for the training of subordinate logoi. There are many schools for the training of planetary logoi. Sanat Kumara attended a school on Venus (see *The Complete Ascension Manual,* Chapter 15). Masters choosing this path will study under Sanat Kumara. The initial training is done through a form of higher telepathy from members of the Council Chamber at Shamballa and specifically from two of the Buddhas of Activity who are the core helpers of Sanat Kumara in his work as planetary logos. The next stage will be to travel to Venus as Sanat Kumara did and continue your training there. This will ultimately lead to the cosmic mental plane.

Only 15% of humanity chooses this path of the seven paths to higher evolution. The training is long and arduous. The full training to become a planetary logos, which means to embody a planet of your own for which you become totally responsible, can take as long as fifty million years. It must be remembered, however, that time is not experienced in the same way once you leave your physical body. There is really no such thing as time on the inner planes. There are cycles of activity and inactivity. Cycles of inactivity take the form of periods of contemplation and mental activity. Cycles of activity take the form of periods of active energy direction that serve to impress the will of a given planetary logos upon the Council Chamber of the planet with which he is working and possibly upon other planets in the solar system as well.

Vywamus told me that the goal of the planetary logos is to communicate the theme of the cosmic day with which it is involved to all species under its auspices in the shortest time possible. He also told me that three of the main spiritual qualities required for this job are oneness, patience, and love. Sanat Kumara has been incarnated in the Earth, using it as his body of manifestation, for eighteen and one-half million years.

I asked Vywamus about some of the classes available during training. He spoke of a class about time and cosmic planning which deals with how to mesh your specific planetary plan with the plans of other planetary logoi.

He also mentioned a class dealing with multi-species evolutionary development. In the case of this planet, for example, Sanat Kumara is in charge of the development of the mineral, plant, and animal kingdoms as well as of humans, but not all planets have a variety of species. Vywamus talked about another class that is concerned with the eighth dimension and provides training in how to handle incompletion on a planetary level in cases in which a particular theme being impressed on the evolutionary scheme is not working.

One other class that Vywamus mentioned is a class on the subject of communication and oneness. A lot of time is spent on this subject; studying, among other things, how to accommodate change on a large scale. It must be understood that masters on this path are not focused on individual states of consciousness but on the consciousness of the whole and its responsiveness to cosmic issues with which it is involved.

The main focus of the training on the third path is on building the planetary, solar, and cosmic antakarana, or Bridge of Light, to God. These masters are building the antakarana of collective humanity, as differentiated from that of a specific individual. The work is done in relationship to the planetary monad, so to speak, and also to other planets. In the case of Earth, one such planet is Venus, which is like an elder brother or sister to Earth. From there the planetary antakarana extends to the heart of the Sun, to Helios, the Solar Logos. Helios would then be in charge of building the antakarana to the Galactic Core and Melchior.

In the process of training, masters choosing this path work very closely with the Buddhas of Activity, or Kumaras, who form the core group that helps Sanat Kumara in his work. Eventually the masters in training will become Buddhas of Activity themselves, on this planet or, more likely, on some other planet. This will lead to the ultimate goal of eventually embodying an entire planet and becoming a planetary logos.

As a planetary logos, the master's job is to learn to register and express the will of the solar logos who is in charge of the solar system into which he has incarnated, so to speak. Instead of inhabiting a small physical body, as a planetary logos you must embody a whole planet. Instead of working to improve your personal physical, mental, and emotional bodies, you are in charge of expanding the physical, mental, and emotional bodies of all species and of the very planet into which you have incarnated. Quite a job! You can see why a lot of training is needed. The impression of your will upon the planet is achieved through the planetary antakarana. It must be done in a way that respects the free choice of the beings incarnating onto the planet, or karma is created.

As you evolve through God's infinite universe, you keep extending the responsibilities you are given. When the job of being a planetary logos is finished, you might choose to graduate and move on to embodying an entire solar system, as Helios has done. After that, maybe a whole galaxy and then an entire universe, as Melchizedek has done. You must expand gradually, step by step, your mastery and worthiness to take on the next step of responsibility. Most people get overwhelmed just dealing with their own bodies, emotions, and minds. Imagine being responsible for a whole planet, solar system, galaxy, or universe! This is your destiny, regardless of which path you choose. Each initiation you go through, of the three hundred fifty-two leading back to the Godhead, signifies another level of expansion and added responsibility.

In a recent meditation, I was talking with Sai Baba and I requested his help in moving to the next higher octave and initiation. The first thing he asked me was whether I was ready and willing to take on the level of added responsibility that would ensue upon the realization of the prayer request. This is something you should consider as you invoke an acceleration in your own initiatory and ascension process. The higher you go, the more will be expected on all levels, and the more quickly your karma will return to get you off track.

If you choose this path, you will eventually become a directing builder and creator of all forms of planetary life. You will have achieved the perfect synthesis of *spiritual will* and *spiritual love*. As the training continues and you move toward becoming a Buddha of Activity, you add active intelligence as the third ingredient, which creates a perfect balance with active love and active will. Before incarnating into your own planet, you will serve as a Buddha of Activity on another planet, helping another planetary logos. The supreme goal of a planetary logos is to impress his sevenfold body of manifestation, via its seven states of consciousness and seven chakras, with his will and intention. The training on this path therefore requires an intensive study of the science of impression. As a master in training, you gain experience helping another planetary logos in his work with the sacred planets in the solar system with which he is involved. It must be remembered that everything in God's infinite universe is interconnected and, in truth, one. No planet or planetary logos is an island unto itself.

The work of building the planetary antakarana deals with creating a link to the monad and monadic plane from the three worlds of dense physical expression (physical, astral, and mental). In this process, the antakarana is also built to the planetary spiritual triad (spiritual will, intuition, and higher mind). The final step in this process on a planetary level is building the antakarana from dense physical expression to Shamballa, or the will center of the given planetary logos. Eventually, the antakarana will extend to the seven sacred planets, to Helios, and, in more advanced planetary systems such as Arcturus, to cosmic levels of consciousness and ultimately all the way back to the Godhead.

If you choose this path, it confines you to a particular solar system for an extended period of time. For this reason, Sanat Kumara has been esoterically called "The Great Sacrifice." This particular path is not for everybody; however, it holds incredible opportunity for those who resonate with it.

Four: The Path to Sirius

The Path to Sirius is the fourth of the seven paths to higher evolution. It is the path the majority of humanity will follow after ascension. Sirius is considered to be the higher university. Even before ascending, people often travel there during sleep time to attend classes and receive further training.

It would seem that many of the other paths to higher evolution are more advanced, and the Path to Sirius serves as kind of an intermediate step. For example, I mentioned to Djwhal Khul that I was interested in the number seven path—the Path of Absolute Sonship. He recommended that I take the Path to Sirius first and then later transfer to this more advanced path after I had received the proper initial training.

Sirius is the galactic doorway to this galaxy. It is closely aligned with the Pleiades. The actual star Sirius is a Great Sun. When I speak of Sirius here, I am referring to the inner plane Sirius, in the same sense that Shamballa is the inner plane "capital" of our planet. Djwhal has said that the Great Sun Sirius is to Earth's Solar Logos Helios what the monad is to the spiritual person on Earth. So Sirius is one of the teachers for Helios, who is the president, so to speak, of this solar system.

There is also a close relationship between the Lord of Sirius and Sanat Kumara, Earth's Planetary Logos. Sirius is also connected with the Galactic Core and, hence, with the galactic masters. The relationship between Sanat Kumara and the Lord of Sirius has intensified since Earth has achieved her sacred status in recent times.

There is a close relationship too between Sirius and the Spiritual Hierarchy headed by Lord Maitreya, who is now physically incarnated on Planet Earth. The energy evoked is like a triangle, with Sirius at the top and the Hierarchy and the Heart of the Sun at the two lower points of the triangle. The energy from Sirius is the principle of cosmic love. Interestingly enough, this energy bypasses Shamballa (the home of Sanat Kumara and the will aspect of God) and focuses directly on the Spiritual Hierarchy. Its effect is not felt until after you take your initiation.

The astrological configuration that occurred on April 23, 1994, which happens only once every ninety thousand years, allowed more of this Sirian energy to be anchored. It allowed the Spiritual Hierarchy to anchor a Light Package into the brain and heart centers of humanity and served to light up the grid points of the entire planet. This was an enormous boon; it accelerated your spiritual growth if you were open to it. The Ascended Masters use this Sirian energy for training disciples for the second, fourth, and sixth initiations.

The entire work of the Great White Lodge is controlled from Sirius. Since the Harmonic Convergence and Earth's move into the beginning of the fourth dimension, humanity has been more closely connected to the Galactic Core and hence to Sirius. The fifth initiation is considered to be the first cosmic initiation of the seven levels of initiation that can be taken on this plane. It is also considered to be the first cosmic initiation from the perspective of Sirius. The second cosmic initiation is the sixth initiation, ascension. The third cosmic initiation is the seventh initiation, which is merger with Sanat Kumara and the seventh plane and merger with Shamballa, the will aspect of God. These higher initiations are taken under the influence of the Sirian energy. Metaphorically, it's as though Earth were the masters degree program and Sirius the Ph.D. program for spiritual growth. It also must be understood that Sirius serves this function for a great number of planets in this galaxy, not just for Earth.

The Sirian influence was not recognized or focused upon on this planet until the Lord Maitreya, the Planetary Christ, overshadowed the Master Jesus. Together, they revealed the love of God to humanity. Lord Maitreya was the perfect example and expression of the Sirius initiation.

Djwhal Khul had chosen the Path to Sirius; however, Sanat Kumara asked him to remain with the Earth for a period of time as a personal favor to him, to help in Earth's transition to the New Age. Djwhal Khul graciously agreed and has forgone his cosmic evolution in order to be of service to his brothers and sisters on the Earth. My understanding is that Buddha had originally chosen path number one, the Path of Earth Service. He later changed his mind and chose the Path to Sirius. Sanat Kumara did not choose the Path to Sirius but, rather, the Path of Training to Become a Planetary Logos. Sirius has often been referred to as the Sirian Lodge or the Blue Lodge. Sirius has enormous influence, not only on this planet but also on this solar system.

Upon leaving Earth and traveling to Sirius after the completion of your mission here, you will automatically become a representative of Earth's evolving conclave. There will be representatives from other planets there too. One of the things that you will probably do is to teach at the higher university on Sirius. Many of the students in attendance will be from Earth and will arrive in their soul bodies during their sleep time. Some may come from other planets. Others may be fellow masters from other planets who wish to know more about Earth's form of evolution.

Besides teaching, you will be attending classes and many meetings. Some of the meetings will be formal and some informal. There will be many opportunities for expanded service work, depending on your unique abilities and aptitudes. Since I have chosen the Path to Sirius, I asked Vywamus how long I would be spending there in terms of Earth time, and he said one thousand years. When I asked, "What then?" he said there were infinite possibilities. I could begin training on another one of the seven paths to higher evolution; I could become an assistant to a solar logos; or I could serve on one of the galactic councils, just to name a few possibilities. Just because you go to Sirius does not mean that the process of initiations stops. There are, in truth, three hundred fifty-two levels of initiation to pass through before returning to the co-creator level of complete union with the Godhead.

Sirius receives much guidance from the Universal Core and the Universal Logos, Melchizedek. Vywamus also told me that Sirius receives guidance from a star system called Tulobra. Tulobra is a universe that has achieved complete unification and is from a Source entirely separate from the Source of this universe.

Vywamus told me that of the seven paths to higher evolution, the Path to Sirius is chosen by 62% of humanity. I asked Vywamus what I will be teaching once I reach Sirius. He said it is different for each person; depending on his unique abilities, consciousness, and skills, but that I would be teaching a class on the psychology of consciousness development, with perhaps a specific emphasis on the development of consciousness through emotions. It must be remembered that many other planetary systems in this galaxy do not access emotions in the same way as humans on Earth. The beings from Zeta Reticulum, for example, are not emotional at all and have more of a mental and group consciousness. Vywamus said he also saw me teaching teleportation classes in the future. This surprised me a little since I have not even learned to do it yet.

I then asked Vywamus about the classes I would be attending on Sirius. He told me that I would be very interested in what he referred to as universal bridging. This has to do with what I have called the merger of Source A and Source B—the ascension, in a sense, of the Source of this universe to a still higher Source. I am actually very interested in this consciously, so it came as no surprise to me when Vywamus said it.

He also said that I would be interested in something called the null zone, which is apparently some kind of space-time continuum on the inner and/or outer planes where all that exists is primordial energy that has not been activated yet. No seed has been planted into it by the Source or the Godforce. Vywamus told me I am currently studying this on Sirius. The activation of one of these null zones with the co-creator gods could possibly be one of my later assignments during my stay on Sirius.

Once you ascend, if you have chosen the Path to Sirius, your homebase will be Sirius for a period of time. As Earth is involved with initiations one through seven, Sirius is involved with initiations seven through twelve.

Shamballa, the home of Sanat Kumara, is a mini-chamber of the expanded chamber that is Sirius. Shamballa is like an outpost of the White Lodge on Sirius. The governing body on Sirius is a Council of Twelve. The focus of their work is not just this galaxy, but the entire universe. Sirius and the Galactic Core are not the same. The Galactic Core feeds Sirius, which is a learning center. Sirius is a part of the Galactic Core. Since Earth went through the Harmonic Convergence and moved into the fourth dimension, it has a direct connection to the Galactic Core and more of a direct connection with Sirius, both through its own contact and through the Spiritual Hierarchy. This connection with Sirius was expanded during the astrological configuration that occurred right before Wesak, on April 23, 1994.

Five: The Ray Path

The Ray Path is the fifth of the seven paths to higher evolution. If you choose this path you stay on your own ray, the ray your soul or monad is on (see *The Complete Ascension Manual,* Chapter 10). Choosing this path means you work under the Lord of the World, Sanat Kumara, and the chohan governing your particular ray. If you choose this path, you travel to every part of the solar system in your service work.

It is a very complex path that requires an understanding of intricate mathematics and the ability to use geometry in a manner incomprehensible to the linear human brain. This path is chosen if you find the law of vibration of profound importance. In later stages of this path, you will serve on another planet corresponding to your own soul or monadic ray. This is true unless you are a third-ray soul or monad, which means that you will remain in service to the Earth.

In even later stages, you will continue your service work with the Sun and work with Helios. Having thus mastered the Law of Vibration in the solar system, you will then pass on to the galactic levels of consciousness and service. It is at that stage that you pass from your own ray and move on to a corresponding cosmic ray. The subrays the initiates have been on are only subsidiary rays of one of the cosmic rays. For example, this solar system is a second-ray solar system, but other solar systems within this galaxy are likely to be on one of the other of the seven rays.

Each of the seven ray lords, or chohans, has certain qualities to express and certain aspects of life to unfold and manifest. It is with these ray intentions and unfoldments that you are involved if you choose this ray. Many first-ray souls and monads choose this path. Every initiate is on one of the first three rays—rays four through seven are subsidiary rays of the third ray. If you choose the Ray Path you must develop an understanding of the world of cosmic purpose.

The first ray deals with the will aspect of God. This ray path leads you to understand the use of will on a cosmic level. It deals with the will to power, the will to love, the will to knowledge, the will to harmonize, the will to act, the will to cause and the will to express. These seven aspects of will form the basis of training for this path. If you choose one of the other seven paths to higher evolution, you ultimately reach the same goal; however, this is the line of least resistance for first-ray initiates. For this reason it is initiates of the first and second ray who choose this ray path most often.

Djwhal Khul, in the Alice Bailey book, *The Rays and the Initiations,* has said that the first-ray initiates who choose the Ray Path must learn to negate their "isolated unity" and must study the beauty and value of differentiation. The first-ray initiate tends to be more independent in his wholeness. The movement toward differentiation leads to a mysterious esoteric training in the development of multiple identification. This, I believe, has to do with the development of your multi-dimensional nature and the ability to focus and comprehend many, many places simultaneously.

If you are a second-ray initiate who chooses the Ray Path, you must learn to negate your "attractive and magnetic tendencies" and learn the meaning of "isolated intention with a multiplicity of goals." The attractive and magnetic quality is the key attribute of the second-ray initiate. You must learn to develop the abilities of all the rays as you move into your cosmic evolution. If you are a second-ray initiate, the exclusiveness has to become an inclusiveness in a much larger and greater world of God-realization. (In such exclusiveness, there is no aspect of separation, as the word commonly implies amongst humanity.)

The training given on this path will lead you to a sacred planet or to some other solar system that will correspond with Shamballa on this planet, where the Will of God is anchored. The goal you eventually reach is a sphere of activity where "sublime purposes and divine intentions" are worked on under the guidance of cosmic intelligence.

Six: The Path on which the Solar Logos Himself is Found

The Path on which the Solar Logos Himself is Found deals with the training process to become a solar logos. This path is different from the third path, which trains you to become a planetary logos. Whereas the previous five paths included a period of intermediate work on the Earth or on Sirius, the sixth path leads directly to cosmic planes of consciousness.

The Solar Logos for this solar system is Helios. Sanat Kumara, the Planetary Logos of Earth, might be considered a disciple of Helios, just as you, as an initiate, are a disciple of Sanat Kumara. In this regard, Sanat Kumara has begun to take on certain cosmic responsibilities, just as humans have begun to take on certain planetary responsibilities.

Certain masters of a very high initiation from the previous solar system form an esoteric group around Helios and help him in his work. The real home of these great beings is on the cosmic Buddhic plane. Again, there are seven cosmic planes, but Earthlings deal only with the first one, the cosmic physical plane. Humans are evolving through only the seven sublevels of this first cosmic plane. The next six, moving in order up toward the Godhead, are the cosmic astral, cosmic mental, cosmic Buddhic, cosmic atmic, cosmic monadic, and cosmic logoic.

One of the main jobs, or focuses, of Helios is the development of cosmic vision, or the development of the cosmic third eye. The small group of high-level initiates who work with Helios form, esoterically, the "pupil of his cosmic third eye."

There are only a few initiates who choose this path and who are qualified to take this path. Gradually, over eons of time, certain masters have qualified and have taken the place of the original members of the group, allowing those great beings to move on to even higher levels of cosmic evolution. The great beings move on to a cosmic center around which Earth's system and even the great system of Sirius revolve. Only an occasional initiate has the necessary qualifications, for it involves a certain type of response to cosmic vibration. It requires a specialization in inner sight and the development of a certain degree of cosmic vision.

Interestingly enough, more devas and angels pass on to the Path of the Solar Logos than do humans. Human beings in the past have passed on to it via the devic evolution, which can be entered by transference to the Ray Path. Djwhal Khul, in the Alice Bailey book *The Rays and the Initiations,* said that it is on the Ray Path that the two evolutions can merge, and from the Ray Path the sixth path can be entered. In more recent times, however, special dispensations have been received which allow an initiate to pass directly on to the Path of the Solar Logos without entering the devic or angelic evolution.

If you are an initiate choosing this path, you are in training to become a solar logos eventually. Sanat Kumara is one example of this, but it is not necessarily true of all planetary logoi. Some planetary logoi of other planets do not automatically desire to become solar logoi. Vywamus told me a very interesting thing: Sanat Kumara has been considering the possibility of leaving the position of Planetary Logos of Earth and letting another planetary logos take his place. He has been with the Earth now for over 18.5 million years; from the perspective of humanity, this is an incredibly long period of time, although from a cosmic perspective he is a very young planetary logos.

This sixth path is one on which, as an initiate, you work a great deal with angels. Eventually you are allowed to enter the Council Chambers of the Sacred Planets before progressing into the group that works directly with the Solar Logos. To reach this level of work can take incredible amounts of time, from humanity's perspective. When a master finally achieves this level, he is given the cosmic responsibility of becoming the custodian and distributing agent for certain energetic principles. For example, Venus was originally the custodian of the principle of Mind, which was brought to Earth from Venus by Helios, Sanat Kumara, and his fellow Kumara brothers as a pure gift to embryonic humanity.

In a similar way, if you are an initiate treading this path, you will eventually distribute other such energetic principles throughout the solar system and cosmos under the guidance of the Solar Logos, until your training is complete and you are ready to take on the cosmic responsibilities of embodying an embryonic solar system.

Seven: The Path of Absolute Sonship

The Path of Absolute Sonship is the seventh of the seven paths to higher evolution. It is the path leading to the sonship of a cosmic being higher even than Earth's Solar Logos, Helios. This path forms a triangle between the Planetary Logos, Sanat Kumara; the Solar Logos, Helios; and a cosmic being that has been referred to as "the one about whom naught may be said." This path also relates our Solar System to the constellation of the Great Bear.

Djwhal Khul, in the Alice Bailey book *The Rays and the Initiations,* has said that there is another triangular formation composed of "one stream of energy emanating from the Great Bear, another stream of energy issuing from the Heart of the Sun or from our Solar Logos, and the baseline constituted of the seven streams of energy which come from our Seven Sacred Planets." This triangle produces the relationship between Earth and her solar system, galaxy, and universe. Its purpose is to help this solar system bring the non-sacred planets to the point of spiritual liberation. Sacred status for a planet might be considered to be when it takes its third initiation. It is through this triangular formation that all the great avatars enter this system. Sai Baba is one example.

In a personal conversation I had with Djwhal Khul, I told him that of all the seven paths to higher evolution, I was most attracted to this seventh path. His guidance for me was that I should first take the Path to Sirius in order to get the proper preliminary training. Then later, it would be possible to transfer over to this path if it is still my desire to do so at that time.

I pass this information on to you, for I believe it applies to many of the advanced paths to higher evolution.

Summation of the Seven Paths to Higher Evolution

The material I have presented in this chapter is a little esoteric in nature and needs to be grasped with your right-brain as much as with your left-brain. The seven paths to higher evolution deal with cosmic levels of reality that are nonlinear and, in truth, extremely difficult to explain, no matter what your level of spiritual development.

I have attempted to give you some basic information so that you have enough understanding to begin to think about your choice. The most important thing to remember is what Djwhal Khul has said in *The Rays and the Initiations:* "I should, however, remind you that every effort to live rightly, beautifully, and usefully, to control the mind and to achieve loving understanding, lays the foundation for the right decision at the sixth initiation." Your monad already knows the right path for you. It is just a matter of tuning into your inner guidance.

The rapid development of humanity, even since the early parts of the twentieth century when the Alice Bailey books were written, has changed the Hierarchy's views of the seven paths of evolution for humanity. Humankind is no longer entering cosmic evolution blindly; the decision is being made much more consciously, with open eyes and based upon true revelation. The mental and intuitive development of humanity is so much greater than it was in the past. Love and intelligence distinguished the masters until three hundred years ago; love, intelligence, and will now distinguish humanity. It was only in the twentieth century that the information on the seven paths to higher evolution was even revealed to human consciousness in written form.

One other important factor in understanding the paths to higher evolution is to understand that the seven paths become four paths, owing to the fact that the solar system in which Earth resides is of the fourth order.

Djwhal Khul, in *The Rays and the Initiations*, says the seven paths to higher evolution merge in the following manner: the initiates upon path one "fight their way onto path six; the initiates upon path two "alchemize themselves" onto path seven; the initiates upon path four have a free range of options.

Those initiates who have not achieved full mental development but are more emotionally-based must pass to the sun Sirius, there to undergo tremendous mental stimulation, for Sirius is the emanating source of Mind. In hierarchical terms, that position is referred to as being a lord of compassion rather than a master of wisdom. One is not better than the other is, for the ideal is always balance. The masses of humanity are still astrally-based, however, and are still Atlantean in nature. Again, over 60% of humanity has chosen the Path to Sirius, the training ground and prep school for some of the other, more advanced paths.

The following chart might be helpful in consolidating some of the esoteric information presented in this chapter. It is my heartfelt hope and prayer that this chapter has shed some light for you on this most mind-expanding subject.

The Seven Paths to Higher Evolution

This chart is from the Alice Bailey book *The Rays and the Initiations*, pages 426–427. I am very grateful to Alice Bailey for her groundbreaking work in this area.

One: The Path of Earth Service

Attributes	Wise compassion
Source	Constellation of the Dragon, via Libra
Method	Twelve cosmic identifications
Hierarchy	The sixth
Symbol	A green dragon issuing from the center of a blazing Sun; behind the sun and

	overtopping it can be seen two pillars on either side of a closed door
Quality gained	Luminosity

Two: The Path of Magnetic Work

Attributes	Responsiveness to heat and knowledge of rhythm
Source	An unknown constellation, via Gemini
Method	The entering of the burning-ground
Hierarchy	The third and fourth
Symbol	A funeral pyre, four torches, and a fivefold star mounting toward the sun
Quality gained	Electrical velocity

Three: The Path of Training to Become a Planetary Logos

Attributes	Cosmic vision, devic hearing, and psychic correlation
Source	Betelgeuse, via Sagittarius
Method	Prismatic identification
Hierarchy	The fifth
Symbol	A colored cross with a star at the center and backed by a blazing sun surmounted by a Sensa word
Quality gained	Cosmic etheric vision or septenary clairvoyance

Path Four: The Path to Sirius

Attributes	Cosmic rapture and rhythmic bliss
Source	Sirius via the sun, which veils a zodiacal sign
Method	Duplex rotary motion and rhythmic dancing upon the square

Hierarchy	Veiled by the numbers 14 and 17
Symbol	Two wheels of electric fire, revolving around an orange cross, with an emerald at the center
Quality gained	Unrevealed

Path Five: The Ray Path

Attributes	A sense of cosmic direction
Source	The Pole Star via Aquarius
Method	A process of electrical insulation and the imprisonment of polar magnetism
Hierarchy	The first and the second
Symbol	Five balls of fire enclosed within a sphere; sphere is formed of a serpent inscribed with the mantra of insulation
Quality gained	Cosmic stability and magnetic equilibrium

Path Six: The Path on which the Solar Logos Himself is Found

Not given	Not given

Path Seven: The Path of Absolute Sonship

Not given	Not given

I would like to take this opportunity to acknowledge Alice Bailey and her extensive work. Hers is the first material about the seven paths to higher evolution ever made available to humanity in written form. The foregoing chart is from *The Rays and the Initiations,* which I used along with *Initiation, Human and Solar*, in the preparation of this chapter. The material from these books provided a basic understanding that was then supplemented by channelings from Djwhal Khul and Vywamus. For more information on the seven paths to higher evolution, I highly recommend these two books.

11

My Spiritual Mission and Purpose
by Dr Joshua David Stone

My Spiritual mission and purpose is a multifaceted process. Spirit and the inner plane Ascended Masters have asked myself and Wistancia (married since 1998), to anchor onto the Earth an inner plane Ashram and Spiritual/Psychological/Physical/Earthly Teaching and Healing Academy! This Academy is called the Melchizedek Synthesis Light Academy! We are overlighted in this mission by Melchizedek, the Mahatma, Archangel Metatron, the Inner Plane Ascended Master Djwhal Khul, and a large group of Ascended Masters and Angels such as the Divine Mother, Archangel Michael, Archangel Gabriel, Sai Baba, Vywamus, the Lord of Arcturus, Lord Buddha, Lord Maitreya, Mother Mary, Quan Yin, El Morya, Kuthumi, Serapis Bey, Paul the Venetian, Master Hilarion, Sananda, Lady Portia and Saint Germain, and a great many others who we like to call the "Core Group"!

I have also been asked by the inner plane Ascended Master Djwhal Khul, who again wrote the Alice Bailey books, and was also involved in the Theosophical Movement, to take over his inner plane Ashram when he moves on to his next Cosmic Position, in the not too distant future.

Djwhal holds Spiritual Leadership over what is called the inner plane Second Ray Synthesis Ashram. On the inner plane the Second Ray Department is a gigantic three story building complex with vast gardens.

The Ascended Master Djwhal Khul runs the first floor of the Second Ray Department in the Spiritual Hierarchy. Master Kuthumi, the Chohan of the Second Ray, runs the second floor. Lord Maitreya the Planetary Christ runs the third floor! When Djwhal Khul leaves for his next Cosmic Position, I will be taking over this first floor Department. The Second Ray Department is focused on the "Spiritual Education" of all lightworkers on Earth and is the Planetary Ray of the Love/Wisdom of God. What is unique, however, about the Synthesis Ashram is that it has a unique mission and purpose which is to help lightworkers perfectly master and integrate all 12 Planetary Rays which is one of the reasons I love this particular Spiritual leadership position and assignment so much! For this has been a great mission and focus of all my work!

Wistancia's and my mission has been to anchor the Synthesis Ashram and Teaching Academy onto the physical Earth, which we have done and are continuing to do in an ever increasing manner on a global level. Currently there are 43 branches of the Academy that have been set up around the world! The Academy actually first came into existence in 1996! This we have been guided to call the Melchizedek Synthesis Light Academy for the following reasons. It is called this because of the Overlighting Presence of Melchizedek (Our Universal Logos), the Mahatma (Avatar of Synthesis), and the Light which is the embodiment of Archangel Metatron, who created all outer light in our Universe and is the creator of the electron! These three beings, Djwhal Khul, and a very large Core Group of inner plane Planetary and Cosmic Masters help us in all this work.

I have also been asked by the inner plane Ascended Masters to be one of the main "High Priest Spokespersons for the Planetary Ascension Movement on Earth." I have been asked to do this because of the cutting-edge, yet easy to understand nature of all my books and work, as well as certain Spiritual Leadership qualities I humbly possess. In this regard, I represent all the Masters, which works out perfectly given the Synthesis nature of my work. I function as kind of a "Point Man" for the Ascended Masters on Earth, as they have described it to me.

The Masters, under the guidance of Lord Buddha our Planetary Logos, have also guided us as part of our mission to bring Wesak to the West! So, for the last seven years we have held a Global Festival and Conference at Mt. Shasta, California for 2000 people. This, of course, honors the Wesak Festival, which is the holiest day of the year to the inner plane Ascended Masters, and the high point of incoming Spiritual energies to the Earth on the Taurus full moon each year! We invite all lightworkers to join us each year from all over the world for this momentous celebration, which is considered to be one of the premiere Spiritual Events in the New Age Movement!

The fourth part of my mission and purpose is the 100 volume "Easy to Read Encyclopedia of the Spiritual Path" that I have written. So far, I have completed 42 volumes in this Ascension Book Series. The Ascended Master Djwhal Khul prophesized in the 1940's that there would be a third dispensation of Ascended Master teachings what would appear at the turn of the century. The first dispensation of Ascended Master teachings was the Theosophical Movement, channeled by Madam Blavatsky. The second dispensation of Ascended Master teachings was the Alice Bailey books, channeled by Djwhal Khul, and *The I AM Discourses*, channeled by Saint Germain. My 100 volume series of books is by the grace of GOD and the Masters, the third dispensation of Ascended Master teachings as prophesized by Djwhal Khul. These books are co-creative channeled writings of myself and the inner plane Ascended Masters. What is unique about my work is how easy to read and understand it is, how practical, comprehensive, cutting-edge, as well as integrated and synthe-sized. Wistancia has added to this work with her wonderful book *Invocations to the Light.*

The fifth aspect of our work and mission, which is extremely unique, is the emphasis of "Synthesis." My books and all my work integrate in a very beautiful way all religions, all Spiritual paths, all mystery schools, all Spiritual teachings, and all forms of psychology! Everyone feels at home in this work because of its incredible inclusive nature! This synthesis ideal is also seen at the Wesak Celebrations, for people come from all religions, Spiritual paths, mystery schools, and teachings. The event is overlighted by over one million inner plane Ascended Masters, Archangels and Angels, Elohim Masters, and Christed Extraterrestrials. Wesak, the books, the Academy, and all our work embody this synthesis principle. This is part of why I and we have been given Spiritual Leadership of the Synthesis Ashram on Earth, and soon on the Inner Plane as well. This also explains our unique relationship to Melchizedek who holds responsibility for the "synthesis development" of all beings in our universe. Our connection to the Mahatma is explained by the fact that the Mahatma is the Cosmic embodiment of "synthesis" in the infinite Universe. This is also why the Mahatma also goes by the name, "The Avatar of Synthesis." Archangel Metatron who holds the position in the Cosmic Tree of Life of Kether, or the Crown, hence has a "Synthesis Overview" of all of the Sephiroth or Centers of the Cosmic Tree of Life! Djwhal Khul holds Spiritual leader-ship of the "Synthesis Ashram" on the Planetary, Solar, and Galactic levels for the Earth! The Core Group of Masters that overlight our mission are, again, the embodiment of the synthesis understanding!

The unique thing about our work is that it teaches some of the most cutting-edge co-created channeled work on the planet, in the realm of Ascension and Ascended Master Teachings. This can be seen in my books *The Complete Ascension Manual, Beyond Ascension, Cosmic Ascension, Revelations of a Melchizedek Initiate,* and *How to Teach Ascension Classes.* Because of my background as a Psychologist and licensed Marriage,

Family and Child Counselor, I also specialize in some of the most advanced cutting-edge work on the planet in the field of Spiritual psychology. In this regard, I would guide you to my books, *Soul Psychology*, *Integrated Ascension*, *How to Clear the Negative Ego*, and *Ascension and Romantic Relationships*! Thirdly, I also have humbly brought forth some extremely cutting-edge work on the physical/earthly level in the field of healing, Spirituality and society, politics, social issues, Extraterrestrials, Spiritual leadership, Spirituality and business, Goddess work with Wistancia, and of course the annual Wesak Celebrations. This can be found in my books: *The Golden Keys to Ascension and Healing*, *Hidden Mysteries*, *Manual for Planetary Leadership*, *Your Ascension Mission: Embracing Your Puzzle Piece*, *How to be Successful in your Business from a Spiritual and Financial Perspective*, and *Empowerment and Integration Through The Goddess* —written by Wistancia and myself.

Adding to this, the 11 new books I have just completed and am completing: *The Golden Book of Melchizedek: How to Become an Integrated Christ/Buddha in this Lifetime*, *How to Release Fear-Based Thinking and Feeling: An In-depth Study of Spiritual Psychology*, *The Little Flame and Big Flame* (my first children's book), *Letters of Guidance to Students and Friends*, *Ascension Names and Terms Glossary*, *Ascension Activation Meditations of the Spiritual Hierarchy*, *The Divine Blueprint for the Seventh Golden Age*, *How to do Psychological and Spiritual Counseling for Self and Others*, *God and His Team of Super Heroes* (my second children's book) and *How to Achieve Perfect Radiant Health from the Soul's Perspective*!

Currently I have completed over 42 volumes in my Ascension Book Series. Fourteen of these books are published by Light Technology Publishers. A newer version of *Soul Psychology* is published by Ballantine Publishers, owned by Random House, which I am quite excited about as well! The other books are in manuscript form and I am currently negotiating with various publishers for publishing rights! My books have also been translated and published in Germany, Brazil, Japan, Holland, Israel and this process continues to expand.

Spirit and the inner plane Ascended Masters have told me that because of this unique focus, that what I have actually done in a co-creative way and manner with them, is open a new Portal to God. This new portal opening stems out of all the cutting-edge Ascension Activations and Ascended Master Teachings, the totally cutting-edge Spiritual Psychology work because of my background as a Psychologist and licensed Marriage, Family and Child Counselor, and the unique ability to ground all the work into the physical/earthly world in a balanced and integrated manner. Spirit and the Masters have told me that this new Portal to God is on an inner and outer plane level, and continues to be built in a co-creative way with Spirit, the Masters, myself, and certain other Masters and High Level Initiates who are helping me on the inner and outer planes! I have Spiritual leadership, however, in spearheading this project, and it is one of the most exciting projects I am involved in.

In terms of my Spiritual initiation process as I have spoken of in my books, I have currently now taken my 17th major initiation. These are not the minor initiations that some groups work with, but are the major initiations that embody all the minor initiations within them. The Seventh Initiation is the achieving of Liberation and Ascension. The 10th Initiation is the completion of Planetary Ascension and the beginning of Solar Initiation. The 11th Initiation, being the first Galactic Initiation. The 12th Initiation, being the first Universal Initiation from an Earthly perspective. Having taken my 17th initiation, what is most important to me is that these initiations have been taken in an "integrated manner," for, in truth, the Masters told me that they are not really into Ascension, which may surprise a great many lightworkers. The Masters are into "*Integrated* Ascension"! There are many lightworkers taking initiations, but many are not doing so in an integrated and balanced manner! They are taking them on a Spiritual level, but they are not being properly integrated into the mental and emotional bodies or psychological level properly. They are also not transcending negative ego/fear-based thinking and feeling, and properly balancing their four-body system. They are also not integrating their initiations fully into the Physical/Earthly level, addressing such things as: Healing, Grounding their Missions, Finding their Puzzle Piece Mission and Purpose, Prosperity Consciousness and Financial and Earthly Success, Integrating the God/Goddess, Embracing the Earth Mother and the Nature Kingdom, Properly Integrating into Third-Dimensional Society and Civilization in terms of the focus of their Service Mission. This is just mentioned as a very loving reminder of the importance of an integrated and balanced approach to one's Spiritual Path. The grace to have been able to take these 17 major initiations and be able to have completed my Planetary Ascension process and to have moved deeply into my Cosmic Ascension process, I give to GOD, Christ, the Holy Spirit, Melchizedek, the Mahatma, Archangel Metatron, and the Core Group of Masters I work with. I have dedicated myself and my life to GOD and the Masters' service, and I have humbly attempted to share everything I know, have used, and have done in my Spiritual path and Ascension process with all of you, my Beloved Readers!

Melchizedek, the Universal Logos, has also inwardly told me, that because of the Cosmic work I am involved with, that I have taken on the Spiritual assignment of being one of the "12 Prophets of Melchizedek on Earth." I am very humbled to serve in this capacity. For Melchizedek is the Universal Logos, who is like the President of our entire Universe. In truth, all Religions and Spiritual teachings have their source in Melchizedek and in the Great Ancient Order of Melchizedek. It is my great honor and privilege to serve GOD and Melchizedek in this capacity. This is something I have never spoken of before, although I have known of this for many, many years. I have been guided after all this time to share a little more deeply about my Spiritual mission on Earth at this time.

The Academy Website is one of the most profound Spiritual Websites you will ever explore because it embodies this "synthesis nature" and is an ever-expanding, living, easy-to-read Spiritual "encyclopedia" that fully integrates all 12 Rays in design and creation! This is also embodied in the free 140-page information packet that we send out to all who ask who wish to get involved and know more about our work! The information in the information packet is also available by just exploring the Academy Website!

We have also set up a wonderful Ministers Ordination and Training Program, which we invite all interested to read about. I am also very excited about a relatively recent book I have written called *How to Teach Ascension Classes*. Because I have become so busy with my Spiritual leadership and global world service work, I really do not have the time to teach weekly classes, as I have in the past. I firmly believe in the motto "Why *give* a person a fish, when you can *teach* them to fish!" In this vein, the Masters guided me to write a book on how to teach people to teach Ascension classes based on my work. I humbly suggest it is a most wonderful channeled book that can teach you in the easiest way and manner on every level to teach Ascension classes in your home or on a larger level if you choose. These classes are springing up now all over the globe and have been successful beyond my wildest dreams and expectations. When I wrote the book I was so involved with the process of writing it, I never fully envisioned the tremendous success it would have on a planetary and global level. Using this book and my other books, I have really done the initial homework for you, which can and will allow you to immediately begin teaching Ascension classes yourself. I humbly suggest that you look into the possibility of doing this yourself if you are so guided!

One other very interesting aspect of our Spiritual mission is something the Masters have been speaking to us about for over 10 years which is what they described as being "Ambassadors for the Christed Extraterrestrials"! We have always known this to be true! This was part of the reason I wrote the book *Hidden Mysteries*, which I humbly suggest is one of the best overviews in an easy to read and understand manner, of the entire Extraterrestrial Movement as it has affected our planet. If you have not read this book, I highly recommend that you do so. It is truly fascinating reading! My strongest personal connection to the Extraterrestrials is with the Arcturians! The Arcturians are the most advanced Christed Extraterrestrial race in our galaxy. They hold the future blueprint for the unfoldment of this planet. The Arcturians are like our future planet and future selves on a collective level. Part of my work, along with the Ascended Master Teachings I have been asked to bring through, has been to bring through a more conscious and personal connection to the Arcturians, the Ashtar Command, and other such Christed Extraterrestrial races. I also encourage you to read my book *Beyond Ascension* where I explore some of my personal experiences with the Arcturians, and how you may do so as well!

Currently, behind the scenes, we are working on some further expansions of this aspect of our mission, which we will share at a later time! Wistancia has also been involved with "White Time Healing," which is another most wonderful Extraterrestrial healing modality that she offers to the public!

One other aspect of our mission deals with having developed, with help from the inner plane Ascended Masters, some of the most advanced Ascension activation processes to accelerate Spiritual evolution that has ever been brought forth to this planet. In this co-creative process with the Masters, we have discovered the "keys" to how to accelerate Spiritual evolution at a rate of speed that in past years and centuries would have been unimaginable! This is why I call working with the Ascended Masters "The Rocketship to GOD Method of Spiritual Growth." There is no faster path to God Realization than working with the Ascended Masters, Archangels and Angels, Elohim Masters and Christed Extraterrestrials! What is wonderful about this process is that you do not have to leave your current Spiritual practice, religion, or Spiritual path. Stay on the path you are and just integrate this work into what you are currently doing! All paths as you know, lead to GOD, my friends! This is the profundity of following an eclectic path, and path of synthesis! I humbly suggest I have found some shortcuts! I share this with all lightworkers on earth, for I love GOD with all my heart and soul and mind and might, and I recognize that we are all incarnations of GOD, and Sons and Daughters of this same GOD, regardless of what religion, Spiritual path, or mystery school we are on.

We are all, in truth, the Eternal Self and are all God! There is, in truth, only GOD, so what I share with you, I share with you, GOD, and myself for in the highest sense we are all one! What we each hold back from each other, we hold back from ourselves and from GOD. This is why I give freely all that I am, have learned and have, to you, my Beloved Readers, giving everything and holding back nothing! In my books and audiotapes, I have literally shared every single one of these ideas, tools, and Ascension activation methods for accelerating evolution that I have used and come to understand. My Beloved Readers, these tools and methods found in my books and on the audiotapes will "blow your mind as to their effectiveness," in terms of how profound, and easy to use they are! I would highly recommend that all lightworkers obtain the 13 Ascension Activation Meditation tapes I have put together for this purpose. Most of them were taped at the Wesak Celebrations with 1500 to 2000 people in attendance, with over one million inner plane Ascended Masters, Archangels and Angels, Elohim Masters, and Christed Extraterrestrials in attendance, under the Wesak full moon and the mountain of Mt Shasta. You can only imagine the power, love, and effectiveness of these Ascension activation audiotapes. I recommend getting all 13 tapes and working with one tape every day or every other day! I personally guarantee you that these tapes will accelerate your Spiritual evolution a thousandfold! You can find them in the information packets and on our Website. They are only available from the Academy! Trust me on this, the combination of reading my books, Wistancia's book, and working with these audio ascension activation tapes, will accelerate your Spiritual evolution beyond your wildest dreams and imagination!

One other extremely important part of my mission, which is a tremendous Spiritual passion of mine, is the training of lightworkers on earth in the area of Spiritual/Christ/Buddha thinking and negative ego/separative/fear-based thinking! These are the only two ways of thinking in the world, and each person thinks with one, the other, or a combination of both. If a person does not learn how to transcend negative ego thinking and feeling, it will end up, over time, corrupting every aspect of their lives including all channeling work, Spiritual teaching, and even healing work! One cannot be wrong with self and right with GOD. This is because our thoughts create our reality, as we all know! I cannot recommend more highly that every person reading this book, read my other books: *Soul Psychology, The Golden Book of Melchizedek: How to Become an Integrated Christ/Buddha in this Lifetime*, and *How to Release Fear-Based Thinking and Feeling: An In-depth Study of Spiritual Psychology*! I humbly suggest that these three books will be three of the most extraordinary self-help books in the area of mastering this psychological area of life. They are extremely easy to read, very practical and filled with tools that will help you in untold ways. Being a channel for the Ascended Masters and being uniquely trained as a Spiritual Psychologist and Marriage, Family and Child Counselor, as well as being raised in a family of psychologists, has given me an extraordinary ability to teach this material through my books in a most effective manner. The combination of my books on Ascension, and these books on Spiritual Psychology, along with Wistancia's book on the art of invocation, will literally revolutionize your consciousness in the comfort of your own home! The most extraordinary thing about all this work is how incredibly easy to read, and easy to understand it is. It is also incredibly comprehensive, completely cutting-edge, and totally integrated, balanced, and synthesized. It contains the best of all schools of thought in the past, present, and channeled cutting-edge future understanding that is available now! I humbly ask you to trust me in this regard and just read one of these books and you will immediately want to buy the others!

One other aspect of our work and mission is our involvement with the "Water of Life" and the Perfect Science products for the healing of our own physical bodies and the physical body of Mother Earth of all pollution in the air, water and earth. This is the miracle Mother Earth has been waiting for to bring her back to her "original edenic state" after so much abuse. This is not the time or the place to get into this subject in detail; however, I invite you to check out the "Water of Life" and the Perfect

Science information in the Information Packet and on the Academy Website! It is truly the miracle we have all been waiting for to help heal the Earth!

One other aspect of our work and mission is a project that the Ascended Masters have asked us to put together on behalf of lightworkers and people around the globe. It is called the "Interdimensional Prayer Altar Program"! The Masters have guided us to set this up in the Academy in Agoura Hills, California on the property we live on. We have set up a "Physical Interdimensional Prayer Altar" where people can send in their prayers on any subject and we will place them on this Altar. In consultation with the Masters, Archangels and Angels, Elohim Masters, and Christed Extraterrestrials, we have set up an arrangement with them that they will immediately work upon all physical letters placed upon this Altar. We have been guided by the inner plane Ascended Masters to create 15 Prayer Altar Programs in different areas of life that people can sign up for. For example, there is one for health and one for financial help in your Spiritual mission. Two-thirds of these programs are totally free. There are five or six that are more advanced Spiritual acceleration programs where written material is sent to you to work with in conjunction with these programs so as to accelerate your Spiritual growth. All letters we receive by e-mail, fax, or letter are placed on the Altar by myself or my personal assistant. It is kept 100% confidential and is an extremely special service provided by the inner plane Ascended Masters and Angels to help all light-workers and people on Earth with immediate help for whatever they need, should they desire assistance. Other examples of Prayer Altars are: Building your Higher Light Body, Extra Protection, Relationship Help, World Service Prayers, Help for your Animals, Prayer Altar for the Children, Integrating the Goddess, Integrating your Archetypes, Integrating the Seven Rays and working with the Seven Inner Plane Ashrams of the Christ, Integrating the Mantle of the Christ, Ascension Seat Integration, and Light, Love, and Power Body Building Program! These Prayer Altar Programs have been co-created with the inner plane

Ascended Masters as another tool for not only helping all lightworkers with whatever they need help with, but also as another cutting-edge tool to accelerate Spiritual evolution!

In a similar regard, the Masters have guided us to set up a Melchizedek Synthesis Light Academy Membership Program which is based on three levels of involvement. Stage One, Stage Two, and Stage Three! Stage One and Stage Three are totally free. Stage Two costs only $20 for a Lifetime Membership with no other fees required. You also receive free large colored pictures of Melchizedek, the Mahatma, Archangel Metatron, and Djwhal Khul for joining. It is not necessary to join to get involved in the work; however, it has been set up by the inner plane Ascended Masters as another service and tool of the Academy to help lightworkers accelerate their Spiritual evolution! When joining the different Stages, the Masters take you under their wing, so to speak, and accelerate your evolution by working with you much more closely on the inner plane while you sleep at night and during your conscious waking hours. The joining is nothing more than a process that gives them the permission to work with you in this more intensive fashion! Again, it is not necessary to join to get involved in the work, and is really just another one of the many fantastic tools and services the Academy has made available to you to accelerate your Spiritual, psychological, and earthly/physical evolution in an integrated and balanced manner!

I had a dream shortly after completing my two new books, *The Golden Book of Melchizedek: How to Become an Integrated Christ/Buddha in This Lifetime*, and my book *How to Release Fear-Based Thinking and Feeling: An In-depth Study of Spiritual Psychology*. In the dream, I was being shown the different Spiritual missions people had. My Spiritual mission was the embodiment of the Holy Spirit. I clearly was shown how other people within GOD, Christ, and the Holy Spirit had missions of being more detached off-shoots of the Holy Spirit, and continuing outward from there, had all kinds of different Spiritual missions. However, mine was the embodiment of the Holy Spirit on Earth.

My Beloved Readers, I want to be very clear here that in sharing this I am in no way, shape, or form claiming to be the Holy Spirit. There is enough glamour in the New Age Movement and I am not interested in adding any more to it. What I am sharing here, which is being given to more clearly and precisely share my Spiritual mission and purpose, is that which I am here to strive to embody and demonstrate. The Holy Spirit is the third aspect of the Trinity of GOD. I have always greatly loved the Holy Spirit, for the Holy Spirit is like the "Voice of GOD"! It is the "Still, Small Voice Within"! When one prays to GOD, the Holy Spirit answers for GOD. The Holy Spirit is the answer to all questions, challenges, and problems. The Holy Spirit speaks for the Atonement or the At-one-ment! It teaches the Sons and Daughters of GOD how to recognize their true identity as God, Christ, the Buddha, and the Eternal Self! In truth, there are only two voices in life! There is the voice of the negative ego and the "Voice of the Holy Spirit"! There is the voice of negative ego/fear-based/separative thinking and feeling, and there is the Voice of God/Spiritual/Christ/Buddha thinking and feeling! There is the "Voice of Love" and the voice of fear! There is the "Voice of Oneness" and the voice of separation!

I was given this dream after completing these two books because, I humbly suggest, this is the energy I was embodying in writing them and that I am striving to embody at all times in my Spiritual mission and purpose on Earth. This is not surprising in the sense that this has always been my Spiritual ideal and the dream was just an inward confirmation in that moment that I was embodying and demonstrating that Spiritual Ideal in the energy flow I was in. This is what I strive to do in all my work, be it my Ascension Book Series, Wesak Celebrations, Teaching, Counseling, Videotapes, Audiotapes, and all my work, which is to strive to be the embodiment of a "Voice for God"! By the grace of GOD, Christ, the Holy Spirit, and the Masters, I provide a lot of the "answers" people and light-workers are seeking! I teach people how to "undo" negative ego/fear-based/separative thinking and feeling, and show then how to fully realize

God/Christ/Buddha thinking and feeling! I show them how to release and undo glamour, illusion, and maya, and instead seek "Truth, as GOD, Christ, the Holy Spirit, and the Masters would have you seek it!"

My real purpose, however, is not to just be the embodiment of the Holy Spirit on Earth, for I would not be embodying the Voice and Vision of the Holy Spirit if I just focused on this. The Voice and Vision of GOD, Christ, the Holy Spirit, and Melchizedek is that of synthesis! This is the other thing I feel in the deepest part of my heart and soul that I am here to embody! So my "truest and highest Spiritual ideal" that I am here to strive to embody, is GOD, Christ, the Holy Spirit, the inner plane Ascended Masters, the Archangels and Angels of the Light of GOD, the Elohim Councils of the Light of GOD, and the Christed Extraterrestrials of the Light of GOD. I feel in the deepest part of my heart and soul, and what I try to embody every moment of my life is "All that is of GOD and the Godforce on Earth!" In this regard, it is my Spiritual mission and purpose to strive to be the embodiment of the "synthesis nature of God on Earth"! This is why I have been given Spiritual leadership of the Synthesis Ashram and Academy on Earth and future leadership of the inner plane Synthesis Ashram that governs our planet.

The Masters also told me that I had achieved my Ascension in the fullest sense of the term and that I did not need to physically die anymore!

I have also been living on Light the last four years; however, this is not something I would recommend everyone do, for the Masters have told me they would actually prefer that almost all lightworkers live on what they call a partial light diet, which is a good healthy physical diet, and also absorb as well. Because of certain factors that are connected with my particular Spiritual Mission and purpose, living on Light has been appropriate for the Spiritual Mission, Spiritual blueprint, puzzle piece, Spiritual contract and Service mission that I came to fulfill!

The other thing I strive to do in my Spiritual mission is to embody Spiritual mastery on a Spiritual, psychological, and physical/earthly level. What most people and lightworkers do not realize is that there are three distinct levels to God Realization. There is a Spiritual level, a psychological level, and a physical/earthly level! To achieve true God Realization, all three levels must be equally mastered! Another way of saying this is that there are "Four Faces of GOD"! There is a Spiritual Face, a Mental Face, an Emotional Face, and a Material Face! To truly realize God, all four must be equally mastered, loved, honored, sanctified, integrated, and balanced! The "Mental and Emotional Faces of GOD" make up the psychological level of GOD. So, my Spiritual mission and purpose is to fully embody Spiritual mastery and unconditional love on all three of these levels and in all Four Faces of GOD! In a similar vein, my Spiritual mission and purpose is to embody self-mastery and proper integration of all "Seven Rays of GOD," not just one or a few. For the "Seven Rays of GOD" are, in truth, the true "Personality of GOD"! My Spiritual mission and purpose is to not only strive to embody all levels of GOD, but to also try and develop all my God-given abilities and Spiritual gifts, on a Spiritual, Psychological, and Physical/Earthly level, and in all Four Faces of GOD!

My Beloved Readers, all these things that I have written about in this chapter are what I strive to fully embody and demonstrate on the Earth every moment of my life, and is what I strive with all my heart and soul and mind and might to teach others to do as well!

As the Founder and Director of the Melchizedek Synthesis Light Academy along with Wistancia, with great humbleness and humility, it has been my great honor and privilege to share "my Spiritual mission and purpose" in a deeper and more profound manner at this time. I do so in the hopes that all who feel a resonance and attunement with this work will get involved with the Academy's "Teachings" and all that it has to offer. I also share this so that all who choose to get involved might join this vast group of lightworkers around the globe, to help spread the teachings and work of the inner plane Ascended Masters. The inner plane Ascended Masters and I, along with the Archangels and Angels, Elohim Councils, and Christed Extraterrestrials, put forth the Clarion Call to lightworkers around the world to first explore this work, then integrate this work, and then become Ambassadors of the Ascended Masters so we may at this time in Beloved Earth's history bring in fully now the Seventh Golden Age in all its Glory!

About the Author

Dr. Joshua David Stone has a Ph.D. in Transpersonal Psychology and is a licensed Marriage, Family and Child Counselor, in Agoura Hills, California. On a Spiritual level he anchors *The Melchizedek Synthesis Light Academy and Ashram*, which is an integrated inner and outer plane ashram that seeks to represent all paths to God! He serves as one of the leading spokespersons for the Planetary Ascension Movement. Through his books, tapes, workshops, lectures, and annual Wesak Celebrations, Dr. Stone is known as one of the leading Spiritual Teachers and Channels in the world on the teachings of the Ascended Masters, Spiritual Psychology, and Ascension! He has currently written over 42 volumes in his Ascension Book Series, which he also likes to call "The Easy to Read Encyclopedia of the Spiritual Path"!

For a free information packet of all Dr. Stone's workshops, books, audiotapes, Academy membership program, and global outreach program, please call or write to the following address:

Dr. Joshua David Stone
Melchizedek Synthesis Light Academy
28951 Malibu Rancho Rd.
Agoura Hills, CA 91301

Phone: 818-706-8458
Fax: 818-706-8540
e-mail: drstone@best.com

Please come visit my Website at:
http://www.drjoshuadavidstone.com

0-595-20941-6

Lightning Source UK Ltd.
Milton Keynes UK
UKOW041836280213

206983UK00001B/74/A